STORIES OF
OLD CURRITUCK
OUTER BANKS

Travis Morris

Charleston   London

THE
History
PRESS

Published by The History Press
Charleston, SC 29403
www.historypress.net

Copyright © 2013 by Travis Morris
All rights reserved

First published 2013

Manufactured in the United States

ISBN 978.1.62619.316.1

Library of Congress CIP data applied for.

Contents

Acknowledgements

I thank most of all, my mother, Edna Boswood Morris, for the scrapbooks she kept from 1940 until she died in 1993. If it were not for the information in these scrapbooks, I couldn't have provided you with all the information that is in this book.

Ernie Bowden provided a wealth of information about the livestock industry on the Currituck Outer Banks as well as the development of the Northern Currituck Outer Banks.

Faye Barco Hooper gave experiences of her early childhood in Corolla.

Larry Woodhouse told his and Richard Chatham's experiences in the Pine Island deal.

Bill Hollan took the time to research what took place about the road going through Mr. Slick's Pine Island property.

Kay Cole told of her experiences in coming down the beach from Sandbridge, Virginia, to sell property.

Susan Joy Davis. I always thank her. She is the person that got me started writing books, and she is my sounding board. I know I can ask her how something sounds, and she will tell me the truth, not just what I want to hear. Susan and her husband, Colonel Bill Davis, retired, are always encouraging me. Bill has just been inducted into the Distinguished Members of the Regiment (Special Forces Hall of Fame).

My daughter Ruth Morris Ambrose. I should have been thanking her in every one of my books, because when I can't spell a word good enough to get it in my spell check, which is quite often, I call Ruth.

Last, but not least, my daughter Rhonda L. Morris. She doesn't look at the book until I send the manuscript to the publisher to see if they are going to publish it. Then, I turn it over to Rhonda to get it in the form the publisher wants it in. She knows how I talk and can get it in their format without changing the meaning of what I'm saying. If an editor from the publisher edited the book, I probably wouldn't recognize it.

If I have overlooked anybody it was not intentional, and I thank you also.

Introduction

There is so much that can be written about the development of the Currituck Outer Banks that I'm not going to begin to try to cover the details. My mother kept everything about the Outer Banks that was in the *Daily Advance*, the *Virginian Pilot*, the *News & Observer*, and the *State* magazine. She subscribed to all of them.

To start with, my publisher will only let me have so many words. If I could write all I know or have access to, you'd be bored to death and wouldn't read it. I'm going to hit the highlights as I see them, and hopefully, you will find it enjoyable reading.

I have had seven books published on Currituck County, North Carolina. Six of them are about duck hunting (published by The History Press in Charleston, South Carolina); two of those are in their second printing, and one is in its third printing. I published one book myself, which The History Press didn't feel there was a market for, about the long-distance hauling of produce before interstate highways, modern truck stops, CB radios and cellphones. I advertised this book in *Wheels of Time*, and I've sold it in forty states coast to coast and four Canadian provinces. It is now in its second printing.

I feel like I need to write one more book because I haven't told what I know about the Currituck Outer Banks, which I have been associated with since I was a little boy.

Maybe I should start by telling you that my great-grandmother Louisa Baum Borton McHorney was born at Poyner's Hill in 1842. She was the daughter

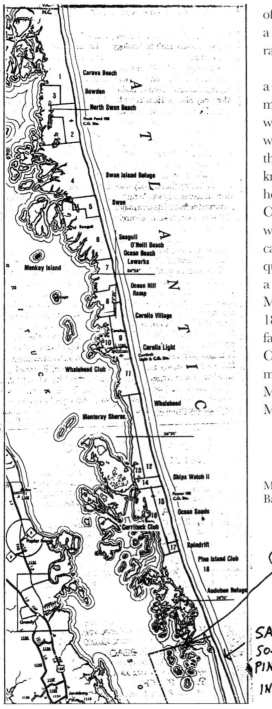

 本

of Abraham Baum. He owned a lot of Currituck Beach and raised cattle.

Louisa Baum first married a Borton. After he died, she married Edmond McHorney, who I've always been told was captain of a sailing ship that went to the West Indies. I know there was furniture in the house that my grandmother Carrie McHorney Boswood was born in that I was told came from the West Indies. He quit going to sea and tended a farm that his father, Samuel McHorney, had bought in 1861 in Coinjock and on that farm is where my grandmother Carrie McHorney Boswood; my mother, Edna Boswood Morris; and I, Earl Travis Morris, were born.

Map of Currituck Outer Banks. *Courtesy Currituck County.*

Currituck Outer Banks

Early Development

Currituck Shooting Club

In 1854, a New York businessman named Valentine Hicks came to Van Slick's landing (now Poplar Branch) on Currituck Sound to go duck and goose hunting. He had great hunting of ducks, geese and swan. He went back to New York and told his friends about his good hunting, and for several years, he and his friends came to Van Slick's landing to hunt.

On June 8, 1857, a group of men met in the office of Philo T. Ruggles, Esq., in New York City and formed the Currituck Shooting Club. Club members bought 3,100 acres of beach and marsh from Abraham Baum for $3,100. They adopted a constitution and bylaws and set the number of shares at twenty-one. The original members were Stephen Taber, Samuel T. Tabor, Stephen H. Townsend, John T. Irving, Archibald T. Finn, Richard S. Emmet, Benjamin H. Little, George H. Fox, Elias Wade Jr., Dwight Townsend, William J. Emmet, Valentine Hicks, Edwin Post, George S. Gelston and William H. Furman.

Some later members' names you may recognize are William P. Clyde, an owner of the Clyde-Mallory Steamship Line of New York (in 1907 and 1908, he played an important part in financing a high school at Poplar Branch; in 1916, he and other members of hunting clubs gave most of the $18,000 it cost to build another new school at Poplar Branch); Henry O. Havemeyer, an owner of American Sugar Refinery Corp. (Domino Sugar); and John Pierpoint Morgan Jr. (whose father established a vast banking empire and

Currituck Shooting Club. *Courtesy Mary Glines Poyner.*

formed the United States Steel Corporation by buying out the steel interest of Andrew Carnegie and is most notably remembered as the person who financed the reconstruction of Europe after the close of World War I).

When Abraham Baum sold this property, he went to the mainland of Currituck and bought a farm at the north end of Narrow Shore. What's left of the farm is now owned by John Wood Foreman's family.

Abraham Baum continued to own land on Currituck Beach and had cattle over there. I've heard my grandmother tell about going to the beach with her granddaddy in what she called a sail canoe to feed the cattle. She said in the wintertime, when the sound would freeze up, her granddaddy would put runners on the boat and sail across the ice. She said he wouldn't let her go with him in the wintertime.

My mother, Edna Boswood, married my daddy, Chester R. Morris, in 1927. He had come to Currituck to practice law in 1926. He was raised on a farm in Gates County, North Carolina, and graduated from Wake Forest College. He represented many of the old duck hunting clubs in Currituck. You will see how it fits in later in this book. With a few small exceptions, duck hunting clubs owned all of the Currituck Outer Banks from the Virginia line to what is now the south end of Sanderlin in Dare County from the late 1800s until 1967. This is the reason Currituck Beach is developed in a more mannerly fashion than the beaches in Dare County. By the time Currituck Beach started being developed, Currituck County had subdivision regulations. The clubs wouldn't sell small parcels of land. They wanted privacy and didn't want people around bothering the ducks.

I think this is an appropriate time for me to copy verbatim a piece from Mama's scrapbook titled *The Whalehead Club: Only a Memory* by Hilda Scull. It doesn't say what paper it was in, but it was written in the 1970s.

> *Scattered about Currituck County's waterfowl filled marshes are plush clubhouses and mansions, reminders of the hunting clubs that saw their heyday during the early years of the twentieth century.*
>
> *"Hunting clubs are getting to be a thing of the past," remarked retired postmaster Johnny Austin, who saw the era at its height and has watched it fade into the past.*
>
> *The Bell's Island, Church's Island, Penny's Hill, and Lighthouse Clubs, among others, have gone out of existence. The Monkey Island Club is now a private family retreat. Narrows Island and Pine Island Clubs began with memberships, but now are owned by single individuals.*
>
> *The oldest club still operating today as a membership club is the Currituck Shooting Club, organized in 1857. Poyner's Hill, organized*

Carl White, fourth from left, superintendent of Pine Island Club, sitting back, telling stories. *Courtesy Ernest Brickhouse.*

in 1867, also remains today and is a very exclusive membership club. [I think she has something wrong here. I've never heard of the Poyner's Hill Club, and I know it doesn't exist today.] *The Mackey's Island that once belonged to the late Joseph P. Knapp is now a federal wildlife refuge.*

Why were men, predominantly wealthy northern businessmen, drawn as if by a magnet to the marshes of Currituck? Carl White, superintendent of Pine Island Club since 1935, settled comfortably into an upholstered chair before the hearth in the living room at Pine Island, explains, "When a man is out in a duck blind, there is always something to look for… what kind of duck will come next. It keeps the mind occupied away from business matters."

On chill November and December evenings, hunters relaxed over a round of drinks as they sat before a fire raging in the fireplace at the Pine Island Clubhouse. Invariably they talked of guns and ammunition, discussing the merits and failings of different brands. They told tales of fine shooting and chided the unfortunate hunter who happened to miss a shot.

"You hear these stories over and over," White said. "Men don't discuss business or politics when they come down here; they want to get away from that."

Mae Simmons has cooked ducks and geese brought in by Pine Island hunters for 38 years. Ducks and geese cannot be prepared properly on a modern gas or electric range, Mae insists, but must be cooked on an old coal stove in the corner of her spacious kitchen.

"Duck should be cooked rare so it's much sweeter," Mae says. After a duck was cleaned, Mae would wash it and rub it in salt. She then stuffed an onion inside and placed the duck in an open pan to cook in the oven for 18 minutes. When the duck was done, the breasts were removed for serving as they were, and the remainder of the carcass was squeezed in an old "duck press" to remove the juices. These juices from the partly cooked fowl were served over wild rice. Peas or Brussels sprouts and a good wine followed by Mae's lemon chess or chocolate pie completed a dinner for Pine Island hunters.

Sometimes guests were astonished at the relatively late hours, 8:30 or 9:00 a.m., when they would leave the lodge for their blinds. "In Maine we go out at 4:30 a.m.," one guest told White critically.

At 1:30 the guest returned with his limit of ducks. "Carl," he said, "you've got more ducks at Pine Island than we've got in the whole state of Maine."

The Pine Island Club was formed by a group of northern businessmen in the first decade after the turn of the century. It's log, which contains a record of all fowl shot at Pine Island and who shot them, dates back only as far as 1912, when the old clubhouse burned. In 1935 the club's membership dissolved when the club was bought by Austin D. Barney. It was that year that he hired White to manage the club and the hunting operations for his select guests.

When White took employment at Pine Island he instituted a number of conservation practices which are still followed today. No gun can be fired within a half mile of the clubhouse, and there are times when ducks and geese come up on the porch of the house for food, White said. Many of the guests enjoy simply watching the birds. White also set aside other sanctuaries on the Pine Island property where birds can take refuge and breed. Over half of the property is set aside as a bird refuge, White said.

White also enforces strict limits on the number of fowl each hunter may shoot in a day and he insists that no more than a half dozen guests may hunt at a time.

"Nine out of ten people that come today are conservation people," White said. "In 1935 they were more eager. They didn't think there was any limit to the waterfowl population." White told a story that reflects the growing concern for conservation among hunters themselves. A party of hunters staying at the club arose at the usual hour for the hunt. They dressed to go out in the marshes, but carried no guns. "We've killed our limit everyday we've been here," the spokesman for the group said, "anymore would be a waste. Today, we're going to take pictures."

The present owner of Pine Island, Earl Slick of Winston Salem, is also a conservationist. Each year thousands of ducks, geese, quail, and pheasants are hatched and released on Pine Island. Slick asks that his hunters use bronze coated bird shot to prevent lead poisoning in birds who eat the shot scattered about the gravel and grasses where birds feed.

Even with the conservation measures taken, the goose population in Currituck is not today what it was in the early years of the century. For one thing, White explained, the geese are stopping in the plentiful Maryland cornfields. Early records at Pine Island show 300 to 400 geese killed in a season. Today the records reveal that the number of geese shot has dropped to 25 to 30 a season.

The attitude of conservation that has grown among hunters, as well as an increase in affluence, are factors which may have contributed to the decline of the great membership clubs. In the early years of hunting clubs,

Mr. and Mrs. Edward Collings Knight Jr., of Philadelphia, Pennsylvania; Middletown, Rhode Island; and Corolla, North Carolina. *Courtesy Whalehead Preservation Trust.*

White said, individuals who could not afford to purchase and keep up their own hunting lodges banded together and collectively purchased lands for hunting clubs. Today individuals like White's employer, Earl Slick, have the wealth to own their own hunting lodges.

Many old clubs have fallen victim to the decline, for whatever reasons. One of the most palatial of these is the old Whalehead Club that now stands abandoned in Corolla.

Edward C. Knight, Jr. was a member of the old Lighthouse Club located on the same property as the Whalehead mansion today. Knight *married, and his young bride, wishing to hunt with her husband, induced him to purchase the property. Women were excluded from participation in the old membership clubs. And so, he built the Whalehead mansion, so large that it could sleep 400 men during World War II, in the 1920s at a cost of $360,000.* [Mr. Johnny Austin told me that Mr. Knight's bookkeeper told him it cost $383,000.]

The Whalehead Club, gabled and magnificent, stands on a parcel of land that was once encircled by a moat. A small harbor and elaborate boathouse remain at the entrance to the property which could only be reached by boat across Currituck Sound, or by a precarious beach route.

When Knight died his heirs were not interested in the secluded palace, and quickly disposed of it to Ray Adams of Washington, D.C., for $25,000. Adams received $30,000 for the art objects alone found in the mansion. For a while, Whalehead was an exclusive hunting and fishing club. During World War II, the property was leased by the Coast Guard as a transient station for men and materials. The Coast Guard painted all the mahogany paneling, and almost everything else, battleship gray and white.

During the summers of 1959 and '60, Whalehead became the Corolla Academy for boys. The house stood empty until 1962, when it was used as a rocket fuel testing station. Today, the property, valued upwards of $3,000,000, again stands vacant.

It joins many of its sister hunting lodges, its past as a gathering point for hunters remains only a memory.

My First Trip to Corolla Island

What Is Now the Whalehead Club

I'm going to start this section by telling you the history of the Whalehead Club as it's been told to me, and what I know from personal experience.

Mr. Edward Collings Knight of Philadelphia, Pennsylvania, and Middletown, Rhode Island, bought the Lighthouse Club property in 1922. Mr. Knight was an executive with the Pennsylvania Railroad; he was a very wealthy man and also an artist, or so I was told.

According to Susan Joy Davis, who did a lot of research on the Knights and the Whalehead Club when she was writing the book *The Whalehead Club: Reflections of Currituck Heritage*, Mr. Knight Sr. was a very wealthy man. He

The Whalehead Club as it looked the first time I saw it. *Author's collection*

took a trip to New Orleans, and it was so uncomfortable that when he got back home, he invented a sleeper car. He organized a new company and got a patent on the sleeper and called it "Knights." In 1868, he sold his patent to George M. Pullman for around $2 million.

During the years that followed, young Edward's father, whose Southwark Sugar Refinery proved a fortune in and of itself, also presided over the Delaware and Bound Brook Railroad, the North Pennsylvania Railroad and the American line of steamships.

Edward Sr. died in July 1892. Edward Jr. was twenty-eight years old. He had one sister, Anna. He was executor of his father's sizeable estate. He started by selling Southwark to American Sugar Refining Company. His second wife, Marie Louise LeBel Knight, was French Canadian and quite a character, or so the people who knew her have told me. Mr. Knight had been hunting at Lighthouse Club in previous years, but women were not allowed at the club. Since his new wife liked to hunt, when Mr. Knight got an opportunity to buy the property, he did so. This property, at the time, was about five miles of beach from Currituck Sound to the Atlantic Ocean with the exception of a few small properties in Corolla Village. There was an island to the northwest of the Lighthouse Club. Mr. Knight had a harbor dredged out around the island and made a high hill on which to build an elegant home. He called it Corolla Island. There were two arched bridges for access.

There were many people employed in building this house. It had five chimneys (the middle chimney is false). Currituck Club only had four chimneys.

E-MAIL TO JILL LANDEN, CURATOR AT THE WHALEHEAD CLUB

March 22, 2013

This e-mail was from Bill Litchfield of Bluffton, South Carolina, whose grandfather was Joseph Albert Litchfield. Bill included in the e-mail a two-page letter his daddy had given him in 1986 about his granddaddy building the mansion for Mr. E.C. Knight. In the e-mail he says, "I do not know who recommended my father as a builder, or how they got together. At any rate, Mr. Knight contracted with my father, J.A. Litchfield, of Poplar Branch, N.C. to build the house." The letter stated:

> *Mr. Knight, who had training in art, drew the plans for the house. He did not, however, include any specifications.* [I have always heard that Mr. Knight drew the plans for that house, but I've been stood down, with folks saying that he was not an architect and he didn't do it; but maybe I was right.] *The plans were turned over to my father to work out the specifications and other details.*
>
> *The site of the house was on a point of marshland. Because of the unstable nature of the soil, long pilings were driven into the earth to provide a firm base on which to build. On top of the pilings, a concrete footing two feet thick was poured. I do not remember the thickness of the brick foundation walls, but I do know they were unusually thick. They provided the outside walls for the basement, which was entirely above the original ground level. The thirteen rooms in the basement are separated by brick walls nine inches in thickness. The house had a total of thirty-three rooms. Needless to say, Mr. Knight had a voice in determining some of the specifications.*
>
> *The eves of the roof are at a level to give the impression of a one-story house. Actually, there are two additional floors under the slope of the roof.*
>
> *At the time the house was built, there were no roads, nor was there any electricity available anywhere on the beach. The only telephone was at the*

The stern-wheeler Currituck docked in Norfolk. *Courtesy Jean Doxey. Her father, Captain Lloyd Doxey, was its Captain at one time.*

Coast Guard station. Transportation was almost entirely by steamboat. A flat bottom steamboat with a stern paddle wheel provided service from Norfolk, Virginia, three times a week. The boat stopped at Knotts Island, Church's Island, also known as Waterlily, at Narrow Shore or Aydlett, and at Poplar Branch. It was an all-night trip from Poplar Branch to Norfolk, a distance of sixty miles. Automobiles could travel along the beach at low tide to Virginia Beach. However, automobiles were few, and the times available for driving along the beach were very limited. All building materials and supplies were shipped by way of the Currituck, *the steamboat that served the area. They were off loaded at Church's Island onto lighters, which were then towed across the sound. Most of the water in Currituck Sound is so shallow that only small boats or boats of shallow draft can be used.*

It had been accepted that no suitable water could be found in the ground along the beach. Consequently, cisterns were relied upon to store rainwater collected in runoff from the roofs. Mr. Knight felt that if a well should be drilled to sufficient depth, fresh water could be found. A well driller by the name of Johannson, from Norfolk, who was equipped to drill deep wells, was employed. The first well was drilled to a depth in excess of 200 feet.

It yielded water with a salt concentration in excess of that in the ocean. A second was drilled until fresh water was found. Water from both wells was piped into the house. This resulted in a duel plumbing system, affording guests a choice of fresh or salt water baths.

Two Delco systems were installed to generate direct current electricity. The power plants, which were fueled with gasoline, ran during the day to store electricity in wet cell batteries for use as needed. [Mr. Will Bratten from Princess Anne Courthouse, Virginia, told me he sold the Delco to the Knights. When I started Currituck Realty in 1970, Mr. Bratten was in the Real Estate business and came to see me and told me he'd help me anyway he could. I found out he knew more people in Currituck than I did. He'd sold them Delco's. He was an old man then. He told me that Mrs. Knight tried to get him to have sex with her with Mr. Knight right there in the house. He said he "weren't about to do that." I knew Mr. Bratten good enough to know if that hadn't been so, he wouldn't have told me that. I always heard that Mr. Knight had a male lover, Dr. Knapp. That is rumor. What Mr. Bratten told me is fact.]

The Knights' house under construction. *Courtesy the Lane family.*

Sand pumped in and leveled around the house. *Courtesy the Lane family.*

Several types of roofing material were considered. The first choice, I think, was slate. I remember seeing some of the samples my father received. I had always thought slate was gray. These samples, however, had beautiful mixtures of varied colors. It was finally decided, with the large area of roof to be covered, the weight of the slate would be excessive. The final choice was copper. That copper roof is still covering the house. [The Whalehead Trust has had to replace the copper roof in renovations.]

After construction was almost completed a canal was dredged around the site. Spoil material from the canal was piled on the newly created island. Horses and dirt scoops were used to move this material around the foundation of the house almost to the first floor level. The yard was graded to provide a gentle slope from the house to the canal in all directions.

Most of the interior trim was done by carpenters from Newport, Rhode Island, who specialized in this type work. Some of the materials used, I understand, were taken from Mr. Knight's house in Newport and from other buildings.

10/15/86
John B. Litchfield

A local carpenter was Mr. Alphonzo Lane who was well known in this area for his craftsmanship. I was told he did the corduroyed walls on the second floor. This does not mean the walls have the fabric corduroy on them, as some people who have copied my work seem to have interpreted it. The wood had strips to make it look like corduroy. The following are some of the other craftsmen noted in Susan Davis's book:

From Norfolk:
John Kelbaugh, building contractor
T.O. Spraggions and Woodfin, carpenters
John M. Wilson, plumber
R.A. Post, pipe fitter

From Corolla and Kitty Hawk:
A.W. Beasley
C.H. Perry

From Waterlily:
R.L. Knight
Thomas Caroon

From Poplar Branch:
W.W. Best
W.H. Walker Jr.
J.N. Garrington

From Bertha, Jarvisburg and Aydlett
Paul Gallop
G.R. Garrington
Daniel Pechman
A.D. Vargas

From Rhode Island:
Mr. Carr

I have heard other local people say they had heard some of their relatives talk about working there.

The lodge was started in 1922 and completed in 1925 at a cost of around $383,000.

Library at the Whalehead Club. *Courtesy* State *magazine, Mama's scrapbook.*

Painting over the fireplace in the Whalehead Club's library. *Courtesy* State *magazine, Mama's scrapbook.*

The building has twenty rooms and ten full baths, plus two half baths on the three main floors and sixteen rooms in the basement. (This is what Shirley Austin told me and she worked there for years, but it doesn't jive with what Mr. Litchfield said.) I don't know for sure how many rooms were in the basement because I never went down there when I was a kid. I do know there was a wine cellar down there. I also know they used the basement to store coal for the furnace. Mr. Norman Gregory had the coal brought from his dock in Poplar Branch on a barge in bags. Mrs. and Mr. Knight's bedrooms were on the west end of the house. There were two guest bedrooms on Mr. Knight's side of the hall and two guest bedrooms on Mrs. Knight's side of the hall. There were two doors between Mr. and Mrs. Knight's bedrooms. She had a door with no knob on his side so she could lock him out if she wanted to. Mr. Adams had Mr. Knight's bedroom and the times that I stayed there hunting, I was in the guest bedroom that joined Mr. Adams's bedroom. It had a mallard on the door. There was a bathroom between that bedroom and Mr. Adams's bathroom. The roof is copper and the pipes are all brass; the floors are cork. The chandeliers are signed and numbered Tiffany. There is also a freight elevator.

Mr. Knight died July 26, 1936 and Mrs. Knight died October 29, 1936. In Mr. Knight's will, he appointed the Pennsylvania Company as trustee for his estate. The Corolla property was put up for sale. Mr. Lindsey Warren, who was Congressman from this district at the time, had visited the estate and was telling about it in Washington. A wealthy Jewish congressman from New York State named Sirovich made an offer of $175,000. The day he was to close the transaction, he died.

Congressman Lindsey Warren knew of Sirovich's death and told his friend, meatpacker Ray T. Adams of Washington, D.C., about the property. On August 16, 1940, my daddy, Chester Morris, who was an attorney, received a letter from Congressman Lindsey Warren asking him to meet Mr. Adams and get him up to Corolla and show him the property. Daddy asked Mr. Callie Parker to drive him up the beach, and he took me, his eight-year-old son, along.

I well remember that morning. Daddy had a 1938 green Chevrolet four-door sedan. The radio antenna was under the running board. I've never seen one like it before or since. I remember it because I didn't like it. I thought it was more "cool" for the antenna to be sticking up on the side of the car.

We met Mr. Parker in Kitty Hawk, and he drove Daddy's car. The road through Duck to Corolla was all sand. You turned off on what is now Dogwood Trail. This road went along close to the sound, and in some places,

The Pole Road from Caffey's Inlet to Currituck Club. *Author's collection.*

it was right close to the water. The best I remember, Mr. Parker didn't let the air out of the tires until we got to Duck. We stayed on this sand road until we got to Caffey's Inlet Coast Guard station. Then we took the pole road. This was a sand track that went along by the Coast Guard telephone poles. The Coast Guard had a telephone line all down the beach from one Coast Guard station to another. When we got up off against Currituck Club, we drove over to the ocean and drove the wash from there to Corolla. This was a real experience for an eight-year-old boy.

In front of the old Currituck Club House is where the beach changes. From there north to Sandbridge, Virginia, it is a flat, hard beach like Daytona, and from there south, it is pebbly. I have a picture in my office of my Jeep on Currituck Beach and on Daytona Beach. You can't tell the difference.

After I was grown and married, we'd go to Corolla several times a summer, but I never had a four-wheel drive until after I was in the real estate business in the 1970s. When I first started selling land in Corolla, I had an old Corvair that I paid $50 for and wrote Currituck Realty on the side with white shoe polish. I left this in Corolla for transportation when I came across Currituck Sound from Waterlily in the boat. Incidentally, I was selling oceanfront lots then for $12,000. Nobody around here had a four-wheel drive unless they had an old army truck. You just had to know how to drive on the beach. Tires all had tubes in them then, and you let the air down to ten pounds.

I had a thing that I could take a spark plug out and screw this thing in the hole. It had a long hose on it, and I could pump all my tires back up when I got back on hard surface. It was just as or more important for the front tires to be down as it was the back because of the weight of the engine. The main thing was you had to pick your places to stop if you wanted to start again.

Now back to the story. (I just thought you might enjoy knowing how we used to get up the beach.)

Mr. Cleveland Lewark was Mr. Knight's caretaker of the property, and he was still looking after it. All the furniture was covered in white sheets but had been pulled back for Mr. Adams's inspection.

Although I was too young to realize the value of all the nice furniture, I especially remember two grandfather clocks because I had never seen clocks like that before. I also remember the grand piano and the big safe with ducks and other marine life molded in it. I later learned this came from the Lighthouse Club. These last two items are still at the Whalehead Club. I also remember the dining room table and sideboard. I learned some more from Susan Davis, and I'm going to quote from her because I think it's interesting.

Old Lighthouse Club, 1905. *Courtesy Whalehead Preservation Trust.*

Mr. Knight wrote the following in the register:

On the evening of Feb. 11, 1925, the iron safe which stood in the dining room of the old house was moved to the new house which is now nearing completion. Those who took part in moving this safe, which was no easy task, it being very large and consequently very heavy, were invited back to the old house for supper, and as guests, have signed the register. [They are the ones I told about earlier as being carpenters.]

This safe is a very interesting piece of work and also quite attractive as a bit of furniture. It is from a sideboard; in the panels are clusters of game and fish. It was presented a number of years ago to the Lighthouse Club by Mr. Freeman, a member. It had been in Mr. Freeman's family for a number of years, having been brought from England by his grandparents.

E.C.K. Jr.

Mr. Adams went back to Washington and made the Pennsylvania Company an offer of $25,000 for the property with a $2,500 down payment and the rest to be financed over a period of nine years at 4 percent interest.

On August 20, 1940, Mr. Herbert O. Frey, vice-president of the Pennsylvania Company, wrote Mr. Adams telling him that their trust

New Years Day 1941. *From left to right:* Aubrey Midgett; his father, Ray Midgett, who was clerk of court and clerk to the Currituck County Game Board; Bob Edge, sports writer; Commander Burke; an unnamed friend of Commander Burke; and Chester Morris (Daddy), attorney for and friend of Ray Adams. *Courtesy Mama's scrapbook.*

New Year's Day 1941. *From left to right:* Jessie Midgett, wife of Ray Midgett; Miss Daisy Midgett, wife of Captain Neil Midgett; my mother, Edna B. Morris; and Mrs. Bob Edge. *Courtesy, Mama's scrapbook.*

committee had approved acceptance of his offer for the property, which consisted of the clubhouse with all the furnishings, around two thousand acres of land with about five miles fronting on Currituck Sound and the same amount on the Atlantic Ocean. I had the original letter in my files until my office burned down on March 1, 1980.

Susan Davis told me she had checked in the courthouse, and there was a separate deed for one dollar for the personal property. That is still done to this day for the sale of the big houses that are sold, furnished, in Corolla.

Mr. Adams named the place "Whalehead Club" and employed Captain Neal Midgett and his wife, Miss Daisy, to oversee it. They were from Nags Head and owned the First Colony Inn, which was a hotel on the oceanfront at that time. They have since moved this hotel to the bypass. Mr. Adams used the club to entertain his friends and customers. After one hunting season, Captain Neal and Miss Daisy left, and Mr. Adams employed Mr. Dexter Snow as superintendent. He stayed until after Mr. Adams's death on December 31, 1957, and he retired in 1959. Gene and Shirley Austin were employed when Mr. Snow retired and stayed as long as a caretaker was employed there.

On August 6, 1942, Mr. Adams leased the property to the U.S. Coast Guard and part of the arrangement was that Dexter Snow be made a chief

Dexter Snow, chief boatswain mate in the Coast Guard. He was stationed at Whalehead Club to look after Mr. Adams's interest. *Courtesy Jarvis Snow.*

boatswain mate and that he be stationed at Corolla to look after Mr. Adams's interest. Also part of the deal was that one of Mr. Dexter's sons, Julian, be made a first class boatswain mate and be stationed at Corolla. The Coast Guard at times had as many as four hundred men stationed there. After the war, Mr. Adams turned it back into a hunting lodge.

JUNE 1942 BEACH PARTY

This was just before Mr. Adams leased the property to the Coast Guard on August 6, 1942 (that date came from my daddy's files). I'm going to quote this beach party from a June 1942 *Dare County Times* that was in Mama's scrapbook because I think it is interesting.

Many Notables Visit Corolla Island over Week-End With Adams

Not Since a Visit of Governor Vance to Old Lighthouse Club More Than 60 Years Ago, Have So Many at One Time Gathered at Currituck Beach, Scene of Many Historical Events; Ray Adams Host at Famous Knight Estate.

Chester Morris, on left, solicitor and attorney, and Sam Rayburn from Texas, Speaker of the House, on their way to the beach party at the Whalehead Club in June 1942. *Courtesy Mama's scrapbook.*

In the party numbering about 20 people were former Governor O. Max Gardner; Speaker Sam Rayburn of the House of Representatives; Senator Walter F. George of Georgia; Lewis Deschler, House of Parliament; Vice Admiral Russell R. Waesche, Commandant of the U.S. Coast Guard; Comptroller General, Lindsey C. Warren; Congressman Herbert Bonner; Representative W. Sterling Cole of New York; W.N. Reynolds, Commissioner of Public Buildings Washington, D.C., and Congressman Graham Barden of New Bern.

Arriving on Wednesday, most of the crowd stayed over until Sunday; learned the delights of the finest fish, soft crabs, clams, and other foods native to Currituck County; and declared it the best party on which they had been in many a day. There was fishing and bathing, and long hours in the breeze on the wide veranda of The Whalehead Club, where many an entertaining story was told.

Bringing up the party were many of the great and near great. They included Admiral L.C. Covell retired, beloved friend of the Coast Guardsmen; Frank L. Yates and James L. Baity of the General Accounting Office; George Nevill, of Mississippi, and George Lane, Business college

Lindsey C. Warren, United States Comptroller General. *Author's collection.*

president and friend of Mr. Adams. Judge Frank Robertson of Mississippi; U.S. Marshall Ford S. Worthy of North Carolina; Solicitor Chester Morris; and not the least, S.T. Cameron, 85-year-old attorney and sport friend of Ray Adams.

There were many visitors dropping in on the party during the week-end, and also enjoying the fine meals prepared by Mr. Adams for his guests. These included A.W. Drinkwater and Victor Meekins of Manteo; Clerk of the Court Ray Midgett of Currituck; W.H. Lewark and S.G. Basnight of Kill Devil Hills; Paul Midgett of Nags Head; Frank Midgett of Nags Head; Frank Miller of Caffey's Inlet; Avery Tillett, of Kitty Hawk; Jepp Harris of Oregon Inlet, who has recently been promoted to Chief Boatswains Mate in the Coast Guard, and Postmaster Johnny Austin of Corolla.

No one seemed to enjoy the party more than Mr. Cameron, 85 and active and full of common sense. He has traveled over the world, educated in the school of hard knocks first, before getting his law license and finally college training. He recalled days of the Civil War when his father was a surgeon in the Union Army at Vicksburg. He went with his mother to live with his father in the Indian Country a little later, and came with her to bring his father's body across a thousand miles of plains to his final resting place at home.

And there was Speaker Rayburn born in Tennessee 56 years ago, brought up in Texas with a family of 11 and worked his way through college on a job paying eight dollars a month. Yet he worked his way as a farm hand and all sorts of odd jobs until he became Speaker of the Texas house, Speaker of the National House of Representatives, and his name is often spoken of as a probable President of the United States.

Governor O. Max Gardner still retains all the fine qualities of leadership, radiates good nature, and regales his friends with humor and sound commonsense as in the days of his Governorship a dozen years ago. Governor Gardner was one of the favorites at this house party.

It is obvious that Lindsey C. Warren retained all his usual popularity, and was met by many of his old friends. A new favorite was Senator George of Georgia. He served as judge on the highest courts of Georgia. There was no end of the desire to hear many human interest stories in which the Senator had often figured, sometimes as principal and sometimes as spectator before he left Georgia for the Senate more than 20 years ago.

And Admiral Waesche made a big hit. His men of the North Carolina Coast Guard were there to welcome him. He found them cheerful, ready and willing to maintain the high traditions of the service. And in the Admiral, they found no stiffness and formality, but he was one of the boys with the rest of them. Admiral Covell [I went coon hunting with him one night] *the grand character who was always so close to the men of the shore stations was equally warmly received.*

There were many others who enjoyed Mr. Adams's hospitality. Among them were the superior court judges who held their annual conference there in 1948. The members of Boy Scout Troop 172 sponsored by Pilmoor Methodist Church at Currituck will never forget Mr. Adams or Corolla. In the summer of 1947, he gave us a week at the beach and let us stay in the Currituck Beach Coast Guard station, which he owned then. My daddy, Chester Morris, was responsible for us getting that invitation. The food we were served and the good times on the beach will not be forgotten.

Mr. Adams had a good relationship with the Coast Guard. He sold the stations meat and entertained some of the admirals and other high-ranking people in the government. Not to be overlooked was Mr. Lindsey Warren who was comptroller general of the United States and a good friend of Mr. Adams at the time. Remember, when he introduced Mr. Adams to the Corolla property, he was congressman from the first district in North Carolina. Franklin D. Roosevelt appointed him comptroller general and his assistant as congressman; Herbert Bonner took his place in Congress. The Coast Guard at that time came under the Treasury Department.

The week the Boy Scouts were at Corolla, Mr. Adams got two Coast Guard boys—Durwood Miller and Jim Quidley, who were stationed at Caffey's Inlet—plus the cook, whose name I don't remember, to come up to Corolla and cook for us and entertain us. We swam in the ocean, and Jim

Boy Scout Troop 172 from Currituck in 1947. Mr. Adams gave us a week at the beach. We stayed in the old Currituck Beach Coast Guard Station, which he then owned. *Author's collection.*

and Durwood put the dory over with the net so that we caught fish. And we did a lot of other things.

Mr. Johnny Austin would open up his little store for a while when the mail boat came. We would go over there and buy candy and soft drinks. That's where I first met Norris Austin, Mr. Johnny's son. He was just a little boy.

Another thing that happened on our first trip was that if we had to pee during the night, we would get up and pee out the window instead of going down to the bathroom, until we found out the water off the roof was going into a gutter that was going into a cistern, and we were drinking it. That stopped the peeing out the window.

Mr. Adams would stop by our house many times when he was on his way to Corolla to talk business with daddy. He would come down Chesapeake Bay from Washington, D.C., to Norfolk, Virginia, on the night boat. He

Coast Guard boys from Caffey's Inlet Coast Guard Station came up to Corolla to cook for and entertain us in 1947. *From right to left*: Jim Quidley, Durwood Miller and the cook. (I don't remember his name, but he fed us really good.) I don't remember the name of the boy on the cook's left. *Author's collection.*

From left to right: Ray Adams, Chester Morris and Coast Guard cook from Caffey's Inlet. *Author's collection.*

Eleanor Adams sits at the head of the table. Standing on her left is Jack Dempsey. Standing on her right is Ray Adams. Sitting to his left is Mrs. Wayshee; Mrs. Covell; commandant of the Coast Guard, Admiral Covell; and Admiral Wayshee. I don't know the names of the others. *Courtesy Jarvis Snow.*

Tiffany chandelier in dining room of the Whalehead Club. I took this picture in the 1970s when the club was vacant. *Author's collection.*

Above: The superior court judges in North Carolina held their annual conference at the Whalehead Club in 1948. My daddy, Chester Morris, who was a superior court judge and good friend of Mr. Adams, arranged this. *Courtesy Whalehead Preservation Trust.*

Left: Corolla Post Office and Mr. Johnny Austin's store in Corolla. 1947. *Author's collection.*

could put his car on that boat and have a stateroom to sleep in. He and my grandmother Carrie Boswood, who was many years his senior, became great friends. The summer before Mr. Adams died, he sent a boat to Waterlily to pick up Granny, who was then eighty-four years old, to go to Corolla and have lunch with him at the Whalehead Club. She enjoyed going there again, since her two grandfathers, Abraham Baum and Samuel McHorney, had both owned much of this land through land grants from the State of North Carolina dating back to 1830.

It was Mr. Adams's dream to develop the Currituck Outer Banks. He tried to get a toll road built from Virginia Beach to connect with US 158 in Dare County, but this didn't materialize. He had my daddy do an abstract of title for the parts of Currituck Beach needed for this toll road. I still have that abstract of title. It was not in my office when my office burned. It was up at Mama's house. Some properties sold for as little as ten cents an acre back in the 1800s.

I got the following from an article by Bill Sharp in a January 1, 1949 *State* magazine that was in Mama's scrapbook.

Teat Collins bringing the mail from Waterlily to Corolla. The boat had a flat head V8 Ford motor with car transmission. It would run faster in second gear than in high gear. 1947. *Author's collection.*

Marcus Griggs leaving Corolla after the last mail trip from Waterlily on January 11, 1964. When he got out in the sound, the seas were so rough water busted out the window in the front of the cabin, and he had to turn around and go back to Corolla. *Courtesy* Virginian Pilot, *photo by Neal V. Clark.*

On Mr. Adams's Jeep, man with the hat on is my father, Chester Morris. Man with sunglasses is Joe Tucker, our scoutmaster. Boy with cap and sunglasses is me. Window above the Jeep is where we were peeing at night until we found out we were drinking it. *Author's collection.*

New Road along the Beach
It will connect Virginia Beach with Nags Head and will open to vehicular traffic one of the most picturesque areas along our coast.

One of America's most varied oceanic wildernesses will be available to the traveler within a year or so when plans of a group of North Carolina and Virginia capitalists come to fruition. A toll road, to be laid down narrow Currituck Beach for 57 miles, will connect Virginia Beach with Nags Head, will open up a sportsman's paradise, and give a new and easier access into a land of romance, mystery, and recreation.

The first part of this new seaside highway (and it will be just that) will take tourists quickly from the populous Norfolk area into the finest game sections of the South. Currituck Sound, fresh water, is considered the best duck-hunting area on the Atlantic flyway and the fishing for large-mouth bass is almost as equally well known (the word comes from Coratank, Indian for wild geese). Heretofore, however, the access has been from the mainland side.

Interested in the new highway group, chartered this week, are Ray Adams, Washington; Guy Lennon, businessman of Manteo, N.C.;

Wayland Sermons, young Captain; L.H. Garrison, President of the Virginia Ferry Corporation; Sidney Banks, operator of the Cavalier Hotel, Virginia Beach; and many other Virginians and Carolinians.

It is estimated that a minimum of 1,000,000 persons a year will traverse the road. And that would be a mess of comers-an-goers when compared with Currituck County's population (including the mainland) of 6,709 persons.

Remember I told you back at the first of this story that Mr. Lindsey Warren, who at the time was a congressman from North Carolina, told Mr. Adams about this property? They were good friends. But something happened, and I'm not going there in this book. I heard at the time that Mr. Lindsey Warren said there would never be a road built up that beach as long as he lived, and there still isn't one from Virginia. There was one thirty-acre section of land, four hundred feet from sound to ocean, where the Currituck Beach Lighthouse is, that was declared surplus by the government except for less than an acre where the lighthouse and keeper's house is. Mr. Adams wanted to buy this because it separated his property. I heard through the grapevine that Mr. Warren didn't intend for him to have it.

The North Carolina Wildlife Resources Commission also wanted to buy the property. They offered $3,000 for the property, and it was rejected. Mr. Adams offered $5,200 for the property, and it was rejected. Then, Mr. Herbert Bonner, who had taken Mr. Warren's place as congressman from North Carolina when Mr. Warren was appointed comptroller general, introduced a bill in Congress in 1951 conveying the property to the North Carolina Wildlife Resources Commission except for the less than one acre where the lighthouse and keeper's house are. It was rumored that Mr. Warren got Mr. Bonner to get this done so Mr. Adams couldn't get the property.

I know I'm skipping around a lot, but it's the only way I know to tell you the story. Now, we'll go back to Mr. Adams's dream of developing the Whalehead property.

He built an airstrip at Corolla and had plans for a shopping center, motels and vacation homes.

His ideas were great but were at least twenty years ahead of the times. By the time he died in 1957, he had made large financial expenditures without success in the development.

You probably wonder how I know all these dates. My daddy, Chester Morris, was a lawyer who represented Mr. Adams. I had all the letters back and forth pertaining to this property, such as receipts from the General

Brochure. *Courtesy Mama's scrapbook.*

Accounting Office for the purchase of the Penny Hill Coast Guard station, Old Poyner's Hill Coast Guard station and the barracks that were at Poyner's Hill. I lost all this when my office burned in 1980. The reason I have this information for you today is because I wrote the history of the Whalehead Club for the Currituck County Historical Society in 1976.

Mr. Adams got Mr. Ferebee, a house mover from Manteo, to move the Penny Hill station to the yard of the Whalehead Club. He had Mr. Ferebee move the other buildings to the beach out in front of the Whalehead Club. Think about moving all those buildings with the equipment they had in the

Boathouse at the Whalehead Club. Note the Penny Hill Coast Guard station that Mr. Adams had Mr. Ferebee move from Penny Hill to the yard of the Whalehead Club. 1947. *Author's collection.*

1940s. He mostly used old army trucks. I had receipts for everything, even the cows he bought.

When Mr. Adams leased the property to the Coast Guard, I had an inventory of everything there was in the house, even down to the mops and brooms. When my office burned March 1, 1980, I had ten of my daddy's filing cabinets packed full that went up in flames. A lot of Currituck County history went up in that fire. Shirley Austin saw a lot of these papers when she was working in my office, but she is dead now.

My daddy represented most of the old hunting clubs as well as Mr. J.P. Knapp, who owned Mackey Island and did so much for Currituck County. As a side note on Mr. Knapp, I was sitting in my Jeep parked on the side of the street in St. Michaels, Maryland, one day while my first wife, Frances, was shopping. This man walked up to me and said he saw on the side of the Jeep I was from Currituck. When I told him I was, he asked me if I had ever heard of Joe Knapp. I told him my daddy was the lawyer who used to represent him, and I was aware of all he had done for our schools. I told him my wife was down the street shopping and that she was chairman of the Currituck County Board of Education. He said his wife was Mr. Knapp's granddaughter and she was head of the Knapp Foundation. He said they had moved their office from Connecticut to St. Michaels and their office was across the street upstairs. He said he would like to meet Frances when she got back from shopping. When she got back to the Jeep, we went over to his office and had a good conversation. At the time, Jeanne Meiggs was superintendent of Currituck County Schools. Frances told him Knotts Island's school had a piano that Mr. Knapp had given them and they were trying to raise enough money to have it restored. Frances gave him Jeanne's contact information, and Currituck County Schools receives money to this day, mostly in scholarships, from the Knapp Foundation. I remember handwritten letters from Mr. Knapp. Daddy represented most of the old families in Currituck County before he got on the superior court bench.

After Mr. Adams's death, his wife, Eleanor Adams, sold the property to George T. McLean of Portsmouth, Virginia, and William Witt of Virginia Beach, Virginia. They leased the property for a private boys' school there, known as Corolla Academy, which lasted three years. The academy moved to Dyke, Virginia, and then opened a branch in England known as Corolla England.

In 1962, the property was leased to Atlantic Research Corporation of Alexandria, Virginia, with an option to buy. It exercised the option in 1964. It used the property to test rocket fuel and make rocket motors. I've been told the corporation tested the rocket fuel that sent the man to the moon there.

FITTING THE PIECES TOGETHER

Sale of Currituck Shooting Club: Oceanfront

Mr. Carl White had been superintendent of Pine Island Club ever since Mr. Austin D. Barney bought the Pine Island property in 1935. Mr. White was highly respected among members of the other clubs.

Kenyon Wilson was an attorney in Elizabeth City, North Carolina. He was friends with Mr. Carl White and also with Walter Davis, who started out as a poor boy from Weeksville, North Carolina, and had gone to Texas and made it big in the oil business. (There is a very good book on his life, *The Walter Davis Story*, by Ned Cline that's worth reading.) Davis was now senior vice-president of Occidental Petroleum. Wilson and Davis knew each other growing up, both being from Pasquotank County, North Carolina.

Wilson told Mr. White if Mr. White could convince the members of Currituck Club to sell their oceanfront to Walter Davis, they could both make a little hustle out of it.

Mr. White told the members of Currituck Club they could sell their oceanfront and invest the money and never have to pay any more dues, and it wouldn't bother their duck hunting. That sounded like a good deal to them. They gave Mr. Carl an option on their oceanfront, which he sold to Walter Davis. This was about three miles of oceanfront. Mr. Carl and Kenyon Wilson got a little cut out of the deal. Now, we take another detour to the Whalehead property.

Atlantic Research Sells Whalehead Property

Kenyon Wilson represented Atlantic Research in North Carolina. He found out in 1969 that they were going to sell it. He and Mr. Carl White were going to buy it with the idea of selling it to Occidental Petroleum, but they needed another partner. So they got Mr. Carl's stockbroker with Merrill Lynch, Stewart Hume from Virginia Beach. Atlantic Research was holding the notes.

Now the deal was that Walter Davis was going to get Occidental Petroleum to buy the oceanfront of the Pine Island property from Mr. Barney; this was five miles of oceanfront. The Currituck Club oceanfront that Davis owned was three miles, and there were four miles from sound to ocean of the Whalehead property. This would have been twelve miles of oceanfront. Mr. Carl White told me they were sitting in the lobby of a hotel waiting for Davis to bring the check. The check had been drawn and gotten as far as Winston Salem when they got word Dr. Armand Hammer, CEO of Occidental, had stopped payment on it.

An article in the January 27, 1970 *News & Observer* by Jim Lewis said, "Austin D. Barney of Hartford Connecticut, owner of Pine Island Club, confirmed that negotiations to sell the club's beach front property to a company involving Texas millionaire Walter Davis have been broken off."

A sale proposal had been accepted at one point by Dean Brothers, Incorporated, a wholly owned subsidiary of Occidental Petroleum Company.

Now this really put Wilson, White and Hume in a terrible bind. They were counting on selling all that property to Occidental. It seems that Davis had been against some things that Hammer wanted to do, and this was Hammer's way of getting back at Davis.

Wilson had gotten Atlantic Research to let him plat thirty-five lots in Corolla, and he called it Corolla Village. There were four oceanfront lots in Section One of Corolla Village. We had no subdivision regulations when this street was platted, and most of the lots were 80 by 150 feet. Wilson got Elmo Williams to draw up the plat and stake it out.

"The Rest of the Story" on Pine Island

I knew the story up to this point, but I never knew how Richard Chatham and Larry Woodhouse fit in until Larry came up to my office on April 29, 2013. We sat down with a tape recorder, and he told me the following:

After Dr. Hammer stopped payment on the check, Walter Davis went to California to a special meeting. He and two other members of the Occidental Board thought they had enough votes to fire Dr. Hammer. After the meeting was over, all three of them got fired, and Davis had to come back on a commercial airline. They took his Lear Jet.

Now remember, Kenyon Wilson, Carl White and Stewart Hume had bought the Whalehead property from Atlantic Research feeling sure they had a sale for it to Occidental. When this fell through, they were in a tight spot. Larry Woodhouse told me that Mr. Carl came to him and said, "You got to help us put this twelve miles of oceanfront together. We're in a bind."

Richard Chatham was the nephew of Congressman Thurmond Chatham, who owned the Chatham Blanket Company in Elkin, North Carolina. He also owned Dews Island Hunt Club in Currituck County. Richard was the self-proclaimed "black sheep" of the family, but he knew everyone. *Courtesy Larry Woodhouse.*

Richard Chatham used to go by Larry's office nearly every day and eat doughnuts (I'm sure Richard weighed over three hundred pounds). He was from Elkin, North Carolina, and was of the Chatham family that owned Chatham Manufacturing (they made blankets). Larry was telling him about the twelve miles of property.

Richard pretty much knew everybody, so he says to Larry, "Give me the phone. I know Dr. Hammer from the Angus days." He grabs the phone and, so help me God, inside five minutes he had Dr. Hammer on the phone. Dr. Hammer was on a plane. He was on his way to California from Libya, and I could hear the conversation. Dr. Hammer said, "I remember you. There were two Dick Chatham's." Richard said, "Yeah, I'm the one that didn't have money," then laughed. Dr. Hammer said, "Yeah, I know you." Richard said, "My friend and I would like to talk to you about this beach over here that you fired Walter Davis over."

Larry Woodhouse is the son of Orville and Ola Aydlett Woodhouse. Mr. Orville was on the North Carolina Wildlife Resources Commission for twenty-six years, during which time he was a powerful player in North Carolina politics. Larry has done a little of everything, from developing land to racing horses and selling illegal fireworks. He lives in the gray area, right on the edge, and he's a great storyteller. His mother, Miss Ola, did her best to keep them all straight. *Courtesy Larry Woodhouse.*

Dr. Hammer said he'd like to talk if Richard knew anything about it. Richard told him he knew plenty, so Dr. Hammer said, "I want you to meet me at the Hooker Chemical Building in New York at 3:30 or 4:00 p.m. Friday afternoon. Can you make that?" "Yeah, we'll be there even though we ain't got enough money to get there." Dr. Hammer laughed, "You want to sell me something for $12 million and you don't have enough money to get to New York?" Richard said, "I'm just joking. We got a credit card." So we made the reservations and flew up there. When we got to the Hooker

Chemical Building, a big tall guy met us down the hall, and we introduced ourselves. He said, "I know y'all are supposed to meet Dr. Hammer here. He's running a little bit late." We got to talking, and his name was Fred Vaulsie. He had a construction company Occidental had bought out, and they had put him in charge of this Hooker Chemical Building; anyway, he looked at me and said, "Are you any kin to Orville Woodhouse?" I said, "Yeah, he's my father, why?" He said, "My daddy and your daddy have done a lot of business together." He said, "My father is one of the biggest farmers in New Jersey. He raises celery, potatoes, tomatoes, and all this stuff. It's a small world isn't it?"

Then we started talking about this deal over here. Richard said, "Hey, we need some help. It's a million dollars a mile; twelve miles of beautiful oceanfront." So he said, "Is there a road up there?" "No, but that's where he [Larry] comes in. Bob Scott is governor. His daddy can get the road paved."

Dr. Hammer didn't get there until after six o'clock. I can see him coming down the hall right now. Old Richard standing there looks like Big Daddy in the movie, weighing about three hundred pounds. The first thing Richard said was, "Where in the hell you been? You've held us up." Dr. Hammer said, "Chatham, you ain't changed a bit."

He introduced him to me, and then we went in and started talking. Richard was really promoting this thing. Disney World, he said. He kept on talking, and finally, Richard said, "You know what? I don't know what the hell you'd want with it if you bought it." I thought, "I'm gonna kill him." So Hammer leaned back in his chair and he said, "Now Chatham, shut up a minute. I want to talk to Larry." He said, "Larry, I understand your father has got some politics. Or you got politics. If I picked up the phone and called Bob Scott would he know who you are?" I said he would know who my father is and he would put the relationship to me but "I'm not a politician, I'm gonna be honest with you, my daddy is." He said, "If I bought that property could your father get a road up there?" I said, "I would say he's got as good a chance as anybody. I'm not gonna sit here and guarantee you, because I can't," but I said, "I can go back home and I think I can get a letter of intent maybe or my daddy can get one from the highway people. My uncle Merrill Evans is the district highway commissioner, and I think I can get you a letter of intent. If it can be done I think we can do it."

We talked and talked. He wanted to know what the hell was the matter with Walter Davis. He said he did things without board approval. He said, "I understand it all, but when I found out he had a piece of land right in the middle of what he was buying it made me wonder what in the world was going on. Somebody authorized sending the money down there, and I stopped payment on it." He said, "I'm gonna send Fred Vaulsie down there. Where can he land a plane?" "It depends on what size it is. He can come in to Manteo or Kill Devil Hills, or we've got an abandoned airstrip that has four thousand feet of concrete right there in Currituck. We need to be close so we can fly the area; then we can ride up there in a four-wheel drive vehicle." Then he said, "I'm going to get Vaulsie to fly down there and look at it." He got Fred to look at his schedule and see when he could come down here. We made arrangements for a date a couple of weeks out.

Richard Chatham said, "Well, we ain't gonna fly back home tonight. We're hungry." Dr. Hammer said, "I never thought you weren't, Chatham." He said, "We got plenty of rooms all the time, and I'm going to send you and Larry over there. And y'all can get a meal, and it's not going to cost you a penny." I said, "Richard, I got to go home. Duck hunting starts tomorrow, and I got to be home." "Well, I ain't going home!" I said, "That's fine; you can stay up here as long as they'll feed you. I'm going home." Fred said he could call and get me on the next flight, and he did. They had connections. He took me to the airport, and I got on the next plane. Richard stayed up there.

On the way home, it was a beautiful night flying. The plane was only about half full. They were moving folks back and forth. They moved me up front. I said to myself, "There's something going on here. About that time, the pilot came on and said the steering mechanism had broken and the only way we could land the plane was with the engines. "We've been approved to land in Baltimore, and that's where we're going to land. I'm sure everything is going to be fine, but we have to do all this. You know you have to put your head down and grab your ankles."

I thought to myself, "You know what, that fat son-of-a-bitch is up there in New York, and he's going to sell that beach for twelve million dollars. And he's going to say, "Poor Larry got killed in an airplane crash."

I had gone to Abercrombie and Fitch and bought me a wind gauge. You couldn't buy them down here then. I was the only one on that row of seats, so I strapped my wind gauge in the seat next to me, to be sure nothing happened to that. Long before we even got there, you could see they had lights everywhere and foam on the runway. When he landed that thing, we skidded, and I don't think it would've broke an egg. And we skidded almost to the fence that goes right in where the interstate goes around, and that's where that thing sat.

They unloaded us, and I said, "Phew! I can tell you one thing, I may have to walk to Grandy, but I ain't going to fly." Everybody on there felt the same way. We got inside, and the first thing they were giving us was liquor. I didn't drink, but I did that night. By the time they said the next plane was ready, I was ready, so we got on the plane and came on to Norfolk. Richard finally got home two or three days later, I guess when Dr. Hammer cut him off.

Vaulsie came down. We picked him up, flew the area, went back and forth and Daddy got the letter of intent saying that if something big enough was going to happen over there that the state would take a very serious look at making a road. Anyway, Dr. Hammer was happy about that. It went on for a little while and then one day, Fred Vaulsie called me and said, "You know, Larry, we have had independent surveys done, and we just don't think there is enough going on to justify the kind of development that would cost $40 or $50 million to get going. Although the Outer Banks is growing, if Occidental invests this money, it wants to turn money fairly fast." So I said, "What are you telling me?" He said, "Basically, I think the deal is dead." I said, "Well, at least we tried."

Where Travis Morris Gets in the Picture

I had just started Currituck Realty in 1970. Mr. Eddie Melson who owned the Kitty Hawk Hotel was also in the real estate business and had an office right across the road from his hotel in Kill Devil Hills. He offered to let me have half of his office that summer.

I was sitting in the office one afternoon when Gene and Shirley Austin drove up in front of the office to turn around. They saw me in there and came in the office. It was their wedding anniversary, and they were going out to eat somewhere. Gene was still employed as caretaker of the Whalehead Club, and they lived in a little house right across the arched bridge from the clubhouse.

We all grew up together, so they just came in to talk. They were telling me about these lots Kenyon Wilson had platted but hadn't sold in Corolla.

Long story short, I went to see Kenyon Wilson the next day and told him I had a gas boat in Waterlily and I could sell those lots. I told him he could pay me in land or 10 percent commission. He told me he'd pay 10 percent.

The first lot sold was an oceanfront to Dick Runnels and his wife, Jo. He was vice-president of Proctor & Gamble. He paid $11,000 for the lot. Before Jo Runnels died, she turned down $1 million for the lot. The lot is still not built on and is owned by their heirs as of 2013. They bought several other lots in Corolla Village and built a house in the woods. Jo spent the summers in Corolla as long as she lived. Their daughter Ann lives there now.

The other three oceanfronts on that street I sold for $12,000, 10 percent down and the balance in seven years at 7 percent interest.

The first person I carried to Corolla in the boat was named Dan Cleary. I had called Shirley Austin before I went and got her to drive us out to the property. The next time, I couldn't find Shirley, and I got Griggs O'Neal to ride us out to the property.

I had to do something about transportation once I got there in the boat. I bought an old Corvair for fifty dollars and wrote Currituck Realty on the door with white shoe polish.

Corvair on beach at Corolla. Engine is in the back. Note Currituck Realty sign on the hill. Albert Bess is there with his Jeep and camper trailer. *Author's collection.*

Currituck Realty office sign on Mr. Johnny Austin's store beside Corolla Post Office. *Author's collection.*

Before I get on to other things, this is a good time to tell you that I got Shirley and Norris Austin to get their real estate licenses and put them with mine. Norris is Gene's first cousin and became postmaster in Corolla after his Daddy, Mr. Johnny, retired. I had a Currituck Realty sign made and put on the front of Mr. Johnny Austin's store right beside the post office and hung my broker's license in there.

For the first lots I sold, I had to get release deeds from Atlantic Research.

Along about this time, somebody came up from Texas, and Kenyon Wilson got Ray Meads to fly me and those people over the beach to look at the property. We'd had a lot of rain, and the beach was full of ponds. It did not look good. Then, I took them in my Jeep and rode them over the property. That was twelve miles of beach from sound to ocean, except for the sound front of Currituck Club, selling for $10 million. Since Mr. Barney had died, this included all the Pine Island property. I couldn't convince anybody it was a good deal. Not long before Mr. Earl Slick died, he called me one day, and we were reminiscing. And he said he didn't know why he couldn't see what a good deal that was.

SALE OF THE WHALEHEAD PROPERTY

In the summer of 1970, Stanley Friedman saw in the *Wall Street Journal* that the Whalehead property, four and a half miles of Currituck Beach, was for sale. He told his brother Gerald about it. Gerald Friedman was great at putting deals together but wasn't good at following through on them. That was Stanley's job, until he got killed in a plane wreck.

Gerald contacted Wilbur Smith with Atlantic Research Corporation and was told that they had accepted a note from J. Kenyon Wilson, a lawyer from Elizabeth City; Stewart Hume, a Norfolk stockbroker; and Carl P. White, superintendent of Pine Island Club for the property.

In October 1971, Gerald Friedman made a deal to pick up the notes Atlantic Research was holding on the Whalehead property for $2.5 million cash. He told me he put the papers in his safe and went to Israel. When he got back from Israel, he syndicated the Whalehead Corporation with James Kabler, Samuel Riggs, Isadore Schwartz and Samuel and Harry Sandler.

Gerald J. Freidman on the left, with his brother, Stanley, holding plans for Currituck Banks. *Courtesy Gerald J. Freidman.*

Not long after this, Jim Pridgen, who worked for Canal Wood in Conway, South Carolina, came to me and authorized me to offer Gerald Friedman $5.5 million for the Whalehead property. Craig Wall, who was CEO of Canal Wood, had told him to do this. Canal Wood had sold a big piece of timberland and had a lot of cash. The offer I made Gerald was for cash and closed in ninety days.

This was the first time I'd ever met Gerald Friedman. When I went in his office, he was sitting on a high stool up to a high table with three telephones on it. He was talking on all of them. He'd put one down and pick up another one. He was buying the Monticello Arcade that day.

He has since told me he will never forget that day as long as he lives, but he couldn't sell the Whalehead property because of the way he had just syndicated it.

They closed the deal on the Whalehead property in December 1971. Atlantic Research Corporation received $2.5 million, Kenyon Wilson, Carl White and Stewart Hume kept around two hundred acres, free and clear. That is what is now known as Corolla Village. That is what I developed for them. Bear in mind, I was already selling First Street (now Persimmon Street) and getting release deeds from Atlantic Research.

Now we are going to take another detour.

THE LYNCH PROPERTY

Atlantic Research had traded the north three hundred acres of the Whalehead property to Mr. Edwin Lynch for seven acres in Springfield, Virginia. Jones Hill was on this three hundred acres, and it kept moving south. Mr. Lynch rented a cottage over on the sound side in Corolla from Norris Austin. He and Mrs. Lynch would come down in the summertime, and I would see them out on the beach fishing. I made it my business to get to know them.

Mr. Lynch had a white four-wheel drive Ford pickup with a crew cab. Mrs. Lynch had a bad back and said it hurt her back riding up the pole road in that pickup. I told her if they'd call me, I'd be glad to bring her across the sound in my gas boat *Rhonda*, and Mr. Lynch could meet us at the Whalehead Club dock. So we did that.

Mr. Lynch had the Soil Conservation Service trying to stabilize Jones Hill by planting grass. O.C. Abbott was the Soil Conservationist in Currituck at the time. O.C. later went to law school and practiced law until he retired. I would take O.C. over there in the boat and take pictures of what was going on with the grass and the hill. I asked Mr. Lynch if he would let me know if he ever decided to sell the property. He said he would.

One day, he called Norris Austin and told him to tell me he was ready to sell the property. I called Gerald Friedman and met him for breakfast early one morning in the restaurant of the old Admiralty Motel on Military Highway in Virginia Beach, Virginia. We made a deal on the back of a restaurant place mat.

I went back home and called Mr. Lynch and told him what Gerald had offered. We had calls back and forth, and the best I remember, we settled on $1,125,000. I typed it up and got Gerald to sign it; then, I took it to Springfield, Virginia, and got Mr. Lynch to sign it. I well remember the day. Mr. Lynch's office was on the top floor of a tall building. He told me that as far as I could see from there had been their farm. The town of Springfield had grown up around them.

If I recall right, we closed it in 1974. I couldn't go to the closing because I was in Reidsville, North Carolina, with Spencer Lingle from Dallas, Texas, getting the Monkey Island contract signed.

Let me tell you a little amusing thing that happened with Spencer. My office is right next door to my mother's house. After Daddy and my grandmother died, Mama would cook lunch for me. Many times, I didn't have time to go to the house and eat. I'd rather have just eaten a pack of nabs and drunk a Coca Cola, but I knew she had fixed for me and she wouldn't fix for herself much otherwise. When she called and said, "Dinner's ready," I'd always go up to the house and take whoever was there with me. One day, Spencer was there when she called. When we got to the table, I was embarrassed with what she had, although I loved it. It was stewed spareribs with thick pastry, not this thin stuff like you get in restaurants. It had slices of rutabaga about an inch wide in it. Spencer liked it so much that he wanted to take the recipe back to Texas.

Another time Bill Hollan, Mr. Slick's right-hand man, was at the office when Mama called, and we had collards. He later told me that was the first time he had ever eaten collards. Back to the story.

Spencer and I spent the night in a Holiday Inn in Reidsville. In the restaurant of that Holiday Inn is the only time in my life I've ever had two waitresses standing over me to see if we wanted anything. Mr. Penn was going to be sure we were taken care of. We were to meet him to sign the contract the next morning to sell the Monkey Island property to the Monkey Island Investment Company.

That company consisted of Earl Slick from Winston Salem, North Carolina; two of his cousins, Joe and Rex Frates from Tulsa, Oklahoma; and Devane Clark from Dallas, Texas. The contract was for $3 million. This included Monkey Island—seven acres at the time—Mary Island, Raccoon Island, South Island, Southeast Island and Lungreen Island. Except for Monkey, these islands were all marsh. On the beach, there was a concrete marker on the south end of the Monkey Island property that had MIC on one side and LIC on the other. That was the original Lighthouse Club property, which later became the Whalehead Club property. There was about three miles of beach from sound to ocean.

After the property was closed to the Monkey Island Investment Company, Mr. Penn stopped by my office with his Boston Whaler loaded with Burgess decoys. He asked me if I wanted some. To show you how dumb I was, I thanked him but told him I had all the decoys I wanted. I think I did take two or three. All I'd ever done was use decoys for hunting. I wasn't into collecting them. He left all the decoys with broken heads at Monkey Island. After I realized the value of Burgess decoys, I collected up all the ones with broken heads, brought them home and got Ambrose "Hambone" Twiford to put Joe Hayman heads on them.

Spencer Lingel was working for the Monkey Island Investment Company, and I was acting as a buyer's agent. When the sale closed it was the largest sale ever recorded in Currituck Courthouse up to that time. How times have changed. If I recall correctly, they were planning to have something like a hunting time share. Mr. Slick was going to put Pine Island in the deal, and they either had bought or were going to buy a place in Scotland and also the LBJ Ranch in Texas and probably some other places.

There was a caretaker house on Monkey Island as well as the clubhouse. At the time, Earl and Mary Baum were employed as caretakers.

I was fascinated with the place, and I always wanted to run a duck hunting club, so I made a deal with them. They had to pay the caretaker anyway. I told them if they would let me open it to the public, I would furnish everything, including boats and decoys. If we made any money, we would split the profit; if we lost money, I'd take the loss. They couldn't lose on that deal.

As I've said before, Gene and Shirley Austin lived in a house across the arched bridge from the Whalehead Club, where the Wildlife Center is today. Remember, during this time, the Whalehead Club was just sitting there empty. Kabler & Riggs had platted and started selling the Whalehead property below where Corolla Light is today. They had left the property where Corolla Light and the clubhouse were alone at the time.

Above: Monkey Island Club in 1974. The gas boat nearest shore is Gene Austin's. The other two, *The Croatan* and *Rhonda*, are mine. *Author's collection.*

Right: Dining room at Monkey Island Club in 1974. *Author's collection.*

Gerald Friedman wanted me to open a hunting lodge to the public in the Whalehead Club. I couldn't have made enough money doing that to pay the fuel bill in that place.

They were letting Gene and Shirley live in the house across the arched bridge for nothing and were paying them a little bit to kind of keep an eye on things. Remember, I had talked Shirley into getting her real estate license. Now she was helping me in my office in Coinjock. The sound was full of milfoil, and we had paths all through it. Shirley would come to work mornings in Gene's skiff with a twenty-horsepower Mercury outboard motor (it's around five miles across Currituck Sound). They kept a car at Jones' Dock in Waterlily. There were no roads on the beach then. If the weather was really bad, she would drive down the beach in their Jeep. Shirley could drive the beach with the best of them. She could sell real estate and run a boat across the sound. If a customer came in the office interested in land on the beach, she'd take them to Corolla in the *Corolla Express*. That was one of the inboard motorboats I had, referred to as gas boats. Shirley could type, keep books and was an excellent cook.

In the summer of 1974, I got my children—Walton, Ruth, Wayne and Rhonda—plus Gene and Shirley Austin, and we cleaned that old Monkey Island clubhouse up good and painted it inside. I ran lights out on the dock. I got Mr. Marcus Griggs to fix the old truck. He had made it a long time before from a Crosley chassis with a five-horsepower Briggs & Stratton air-cooled motor. We used that to haul everything. I also took a lawn mower over there.

Shirley was going to do the cooking, and Gene was going to help guide. The clubhouse had eight bedrooms. I kept one bedroom for Gene and Shirley and one bedroom for myself. One of the bedrooms had two single beds. If I had eight guests, I would have to go home. I tried to keep it to six guests.

Earl and Mary Baum quit as caretakers that summer, and they hired Jack and Sylvia Jarvis as caretakers. I advertised hunting at the club in *Sports Afield*, *Field & Stream* and *Ducks Unlimited*. I had a lot of calls from the first two, but *Ducks Unlimited* was the only one I had takers from. The main reason for that was probably the price. At that time, guides would take two men in a bush blind in Currituck Sound for $50. I was charging $175 per person per day, but this included being picked up at the dock at Waterlily and taken four miles out in Currituck sound to Monkey Island, hors d'oeuvres before dinner, good liquor, a good dinner cooked by Shirley, a good oak fire in the fireplace, a bedroom in a steam-heated clubhouse, a full hot breakfast the next morning and a guide for each two men who would take their guns and shell box down to the dock to a gas boat with a cabin for the trip over to the marsh on the beach side of the sound. The guide would anchor the gas boat out from the blind and take his sportsmen in the skiff he was towing to the blind in the marsh.

About 11:00 a.m., the guide would take the decoys up and bring the men in for a hot lunch. They would usually take a nap and go back out about 2:00 p.m. I would put them in a good blind in the morning and somewhere to kill time in the afternoon. Although I had between forty and fifty blinds, you can have only so many good ones, and you can't shoot them to death. At that time, I had control of the Monkey Island property and part of the Whalehead property. This was about five miles of land, from Penny Hill to great Beach Pond on the Whalehead property.

I got a duck-picking machine and Sylvia Jarvis picked the ducks as well as helped Shirley in the kitchen. Jack was one of the guides. Of course, Sylvia and Jack were paid for their work in addition to their caretaker salaries. If the men wanted to take their ducks home, we would pack them in Styrofoam coolers for them.

The men usually stayed three days. That was as long as I wanted them to stay, because by that time I had run out of stories to tell.

I did have one man, George Brennan Sr., who came every year and brought his son George Jr. and stayed a week each year I was there. When he came, he had always just come from Scotland grouse hunting and would bring smoked salmon.

George was in the rigging business. He was from Rumson, New Jersey. If Macy's wanted a car put on the tenth floor, he'd knock a hole in the wall and put it in there.

Now that you know what it was like to hunt in the style that the old duck hunters hunted in, I'll tell you the rest of the story.

That first season, I ran the club on a joint venture with the Monkey Island Investment Company. The Frates, Mr. Slick's cousins, were the second-largest holders of office space in the country. About this time in 1974, things turned around, and office space was going begging. The Frateses wanted out of the deal.

The Monkey Island Investment Company had paid the Penns a $750,000 down on the $3 million deal, and the Penns were holding a note and deed of trust for the balance.

The Penns didn't have to give them anything, but I persuaded Mr. Penn to give them 155 acres of beach from sound to ocean on the south end of the property for the $750,000 they had paid down. Mr. Slick later took the Frateses out of the deal.

After this deal with the Monkey Island Investment Company fell through, Mr. Frank Penn and his attorney, Mr. Charles Campbell, came to see me, and Mr. Penn wanted me to assist him in selling the property. He told me what he'd pay me, and he paid me to the penny; there was never anything in writing.

I made the same deal with Mr. Penn I had made with the Monkey Island Investment Company as to running the club. I did this for three more years and showed it to several people who were interested, but we ended up selling it to the Nature Conservancy. The deal closed after the 1978–79 hunting season.

Back to the Whalehead Property

Remember I told you that Kenyon Wilson, Carl White and Stewart Hume got 200 acres of the Whalehead property free and clear when Gerald Friedman, et al., bought the property? There were 125 acres of the property that was marsh with just a little over an acre of high land.

Dr. Doyle Pruitt and Dr. Eldon Parks were from Elkin, North Carolina. They had been hunting with Bill Riddick and me in either his or my float rig for many years. When I opened Monkey Island to the public, they went there and took Sid Tayloe with them. He was president of the Yadkin Valley Bank in Elkin, North Carolina.

In 1977, I sold them the 125 acres of the Whalehead property. They brought in Floyd Brendle, who then owned Brindle Stores. They named the club Lighthouse Club after the original Lighthouse Club. They might have brought in Dr. Miller and some others as well.

They built a big clubhouse there overlooking Lighthouse Pond. It had a cupola on top that you could look from and see from Swan Island to Narrows Island. They even had a fireplace up there. They also built a helicopter pad for Floyd Brendle's helicopter.

You have to remember, there was no road to Corolla. Jimmy Hayman (J.I. Hayman & Son Building Supply in Coinjock) had a six-wheel drive army truck and carried the building supplies up there.

I got Gene and Shirley Austin the job as caretakers. As bad as I hated to lose them at Monkey Island, I knew Monkey Island was in the process of being sold, and they needed the job. Gene and Shirley were still helping me at Monkey Island in the 1977 season while the new Lighthouse Club was being built.

Last trip from Monkey Island before the sound froze over on January 10, 1977. Dr. Doyle Pruitt, Dr. Eldon Parks, Sid Tayloe and another man, all from Elkin, North Carolina, are pictured. *Author's collection.*

The year 1977 had a very cold winter. The last boat left Monkey Island January 10, 1977. The *Corolla Express* was the only boat I had that had fiberglass on it and could run through the ice. I had Dr. Pruitt, Dr. Parks, Sid Tayloe and I don't remember the other man's name. When I got to Waterlily every drop of spray that flew was frozen. The boat was a solid sheet of ice. On January 20, 1977, I had to get the Coast Guard helicopter to take Jack and Sylvia Jarvis and her mother off Monkey Island.

The Nature Conservancy was showing interest in the property. Mr. Penn wanted me to fly to Washington, D.C., to go with him and his attorney, Mr. Charles Campbell, to meet with Pat Noona, president, and Greg Lowe, vice-president, at the National Headquarters of the Nature Conservancy in Arlington, Virginia.

Flying up there that day, Chesapeake Bay was frozen over solid. I've never seen that before or since. They were having to fly supplies to Tangier Island.

That was the only time in my life that I've ever been in a room that I felt was bugged. They made an offer that was less my commission; then, they left us in the room by ourselves. We decided the room was bugged, so we passed notes. The Nature Conservancy doesn't want to pay any real estate brokerage.

The Nature Conservancy was also interested in the Swan Island marsh. Later that year, members of the Mellon Foundation, Pat Noona and Greg Lowe, flew into Norfolk on Paul Mellon's Gulf Stream jet. Dippy Pender, who was a member of Swan Island Club, picked them up at the airport and took them by Swan Island and on to Monkey Island for lunch. Swan Island Club had two or three johnboats with little cabins built on them. They were running in shallow water so it wasn't too rough.

The tide was about as low as I've ever seen it. We'd had a strong northeaster for a long time. It was the only time I can ever remember not being able to get the gas boats to the Monkey Island dock. I had to anchor them off the dock and come to the dock with my big twenty-three-foot skiff I carry my float box on. I had to get a ladder to put in the skiff to get up to the dock. I had two of my Jeeps and Gene Austin's on the airstrip at the Whalehead Club. I had built a dock there so when it was too shallow to get in the boat basin I could tie up there.

Shirley Austin was fixing lunch for them. After lunch, I was to take them to Corolla (Whalehead Club) and then take them in the Jeeps up the beach to show them the beach property. They were also getting part of Swan Island's beach property.

When Dippy Pender and the man helping him got to the dock with the outboard johnboats, I put the ladder down so they could get up on the dock. Pat Noona walked by me and never spoke to me just like he'd never seen me before. He just took charge without so much as introducing me to anyone. That really pissed me off. When I got the opportunity, I got him down in that south hall in the clubhouse and told him, "These people are drinking my liquor, eating my food, riding in my boats, and my Jeeps, not Frank Penn's. I can make this deal, or I can screw it a whole lot easier. And if you don't introduce me to these people, I'm going to screw it. Take your choice." He introduced me.

The only names I remember were Timothy Melon, Paul Melon's son; Mr. William F. Rockwell (at the time, chairman of North American Rockwell); and Greg Lowe, vice-president of the National Nature Conservancy. Greg was from Rocky Mount, North Carolina, and I was on the same wavelength as him, but not as Noona.

After lunch, I got them in the skiff and took them out to the gas boats. Walton, my son, was running the *Corolla Express*, and I was running *Rhonda*. Mr. Rockwell was riding with me. The tide was so low that I had to get them ashore in Corolla the same way in the skiff. Every time I did that, Mr. Rockwell would say, "Well done".

My twenty-three-foot hunting skiff tied up to Monkey Island dock, and two of my gas boats, *Rhonda* and *Corolla Express*, anchored off the end of the dock. *Author's collection.*

We carried them up the beach in the Jeeps and showed them the beach. I was later told that going back on the plane that afternoon, the Mellon Foundation voted to give the Nature Conservancy $4 million to buy the Monkey Island and Swan Island properties. I was also told they said I did a good job of showing the property under adverse circumstances. At the time, they said that was the largest cash grant a conservancy organization had ever received.

I think Phillip Hanes was on the board of the Nature Conservancy. At any rate, he had Dave Mourine from Washington, D.C., down to Currituck Club and wanted me to take them duck hunting at Monkey Island. He was going to come up the beach from Currituck Club to the Whalehead Club (remember, that was sitting empty at the time), and I was to pick them up in a boat on the morning of December 14, 1977. I had my son Walton go to Northeast Point and tie the decoys out while I went to pick the men up.

When I got back to the blind with them I asked Walton if he had seen any ducks. He said they were about to come in the blind with him. I was counting on that. I put them in the blind, and in twenty minutes, they had their limit and were apologizing for the way they were shooting.

I took them out of the blind and carried them to the club. Shirley was going to fix lunch for them. Walton took up the decoys. Since they had

Frank Penn leaving Monkey Island for the last time. His attorney, Charles Campbell, is holding the door for him. I don't remember the other man's name. *Author's collection.*

gotten their limit so early, it was a while before lunch, so we just sat around and talked and probably had a bloody mary or two.

By the time lunch was over, the sea fog had set in so thick that you couldn't see the end of the dock. I didn't have a compass course back to the Whalehead Club, but I had no problem going back to the dock in Waterlily. This is where I carried them, and Walton took them in my Jeep back to Currituck Club.

After the 1977–78 season, Gene and Shirley Austin left for their new job with Lighthouse Club. I had to have a cook. I hired Charlene Dowdy's mother. I bought her a recliner chair for her bedroom and everything. After the first day of the 1978 season, she quit. The guides ate in the kitchen. She said Hambone could eat toast faster than she could cook it. I was in a real jam now. I think it was Charlene that helped me find this young girl. She was twenty-seven, named Pat McCleney. She had been a photographer for the *Daily Advance* and had a degree in journalism. She wore bib overalls and drank Old Granddad, but she could cook really good fried chicken.

Jack and Sylvia Jarvis left that summer of 1977, also. I think Sylvia got a job with a real estate company on the beach. Mr. Penn then hired John and Diane LaRoke as caretakers.

The best I recall, the Penn's received $1,750,000 cash and a big tax write-off for the remainder of the property.

JAMES JOHNSON

James Johnson was from down around Lumberton, North Carolina. His daddy was a druggist there. My daddy knew his daddy. He came from a very wealthy family. They owned a lot of timberland, and I don't know what else.

I was told that he came to Elizabeth City in 1971 or '72 with a cashier's check for $1 million and went to Mr. Henry Leroy, an attorney in Elizabeth City, for assistance in making an offer to buy the Whalehead property. At the time, Atlantic Research was holding the notes from Wilson, White and Hume on the property. Needless to say, the $1 million didn't buy the property.

Mr. Barney died May 8, 1971. James Johnson knew that and knew the Pine Island property was for sale.

Mrs. Barney told Mr. Carl White she wanted to sell the property, and I think the price she was asking was $2,750,000. Mr. Carl got with his stockbroker Stewart Hume, and they advertised it in the *Wall Street Journal*. Larry Woodhouse told me the only response they got was from Hugh Hefner. Mrs. Barney said she would give it away before she'd sell it to him.

Now, I don't know if James Johnson saw the ad or where he found out the property was for sale. Mr. Carl White told me that James went straight to see Mrs. Barney in Connecticut.

I NEED TO TAKE A LITTLE DETOUR HERE AND TELL YOU HOW MR. EARL SLICK GETS IN THE PICTURE

From an interview with Larry Woodhouse

Melvin Dowdy was working for the Rocky Mount bunch, Mr. P.K. Gravely and others, that owned the Narrows Island Club property. They all fell out over something, and they gave Melvin an option on it for $5,000. They said, "Give us $100,000 and to hell with the hunting." Melvin took it, and Mr. Carl and Daddy [Orville Woodhouse] each put up $2,500. And Mr. Carl said, "There's a guy named Earl Slick that's been down here. He's friends with Hugh Chatham and Dick Chatham. He's hunted Dews Island and hunted over here at Pine Island, and he told me if anything ever comes up he might want to talk about it. I checked him out, and he's probably one of the richest men in North Carolina. He moved up here from Texas. He started Slick Airways, which was the first freight airline in the country. He's just got all kinds of money. Trouble is, I don't know how to get to him." Daddy said, "I know how to get to him. I'll call Bert Bennett, see if he knows him." So he called Bennett and he said, "Oh yeah, I know him; he just bought a radio station for $45 million."

They got up with Mr. Slick, and he said he'd be down the next day. He said, "Carl, you meet me at the airstrip in Maple." Mr. Carl told Larry, "Uh, oh, you'll have to go with him and show him the property. I don't fly; then we'll take him in the boat and show it to him."

I met with him, and we flew around. And I showed him the whole marsh and the little half acre where the Island was. When we landed the plane, Mr. Slick said, "Larry, who you reckon I make the check to?" I said, "I don't know, but I bet we can find out before the day's over. Well, I'll ask Carl. Mr. Carl and Mr. Woodhouse were trying to get $135,000."

After we got back from the flight, we went to Grandy and got in the little skiff and went out there and stood on Narrows Island. They talked a little bit, and Mr. Carl was telling him about all the good hunting that had been there. Riding back to the office, I told Mr. Carl, "Let me tell you something: I think Mr. Slick knows what is going on. I think he's talked to somebody in this whole thing. He wants to buy it because he asked me who to make the check to."

Mr. Carl said, "I'm glad you told me that." Slick asked, "Carl, exactly how much is this thing going to cost me?" Mr. Carl said, "I tell you what, Mr. Slick. We got an option for $100,000; anything over that, I'm gonna take and I'm gonna split it with Orville, and I might have to give Larry something." Mr. Slick said, "Mr. White, I'm glad you told me that. I had already heard through the grapevine about it, but I love to deal with people that are honest and up front. Everybody is after your money, and I ain't got much. And I have to look after it. Anyway, I got enough to buy this piece of property and enough to give you a job." Mr. Carl said, "Well, you need to rent my farm, and I can put this together. And Larry's got some equipment." We were doing Poplar Branch Landing at the time. They were standing there talking, and Mr. Slick said he sure hoped what happened to him the last time when he bought a piece of marsh in Louisiana didn't happen here. They were drilling for water and hit oil and pumped $100 million worth of oil, and it messed up his duck hunting. I said, "Mr. Slick, I don't want to hurt your feelings, but me and my buddy are doing Waterview Shores over there—it's not far, right over there—and if you find oil, I'm gonna try to hook into your well." He said, "I like a guy that's always thinking."

He said he'd get Paul Mickey to send $125,000 down here. "Give Orville twelve-five, and we'll give Larry a job."

We went up there and dug the ditch where they dock their boats and filled in around there and all. It was a good deal for everybody.

Then Mr. Barney died. Mrs. Barney tells Carl she wants to sell the property, and she wants $2.5 million for it. Carl gets with Stewart Hume, his stockbroker with Merrill Lynch, and they put ads in the *Wall Street Journal* and other papers. They only had one taker: Hugh Hefner with the Playboy Club. Mr. Carl came to daddy's office. Daddy must have had the only private phone line in that end of the county then. He got in the room and shut the door. Daddy called Mrs. Barney. She said she'd give it to the Lost Colony or the Indians before she'd sell it to Hugh Hefner for a Playboy Club.

Daddy said, "Well, why don't you call Earl Slick? He might be interested." So he got Mr. Slick on the phone. He said, "Number one, I'm not even interested in it, but if I was, I wouldn't pay over $2 million at the most for it."

Mr. Carl said, "Well let me ask you a question, Mr. Slick. Is that an offer? If Mrs. Barney would say she'd take $2 million?" Carl said, "I can tell you this much. She is in the notion of selling it because the Playboy Club has just made her mad. She said she'd give it away before she'd sell it to them." "Yes, it is. I will give $2 million for it, and I'll close it in thirty days. All they got to do is deal with Paul Mickey."

Mr. Carl called Mrs. Barney and said, "You might want to talk to this one or that one." She said, "I don't have to talk to anybody. Mr. Slick just bought a piece of property."

Mr. Carl White, who had worked for Mr. Barney as superintendent of Pine Island

Mr. and Mrs. Earl Slick leaving Narrows Island. *Courtesy, Phyllis S. Cowell.*

Pine Island Club. *Courtesy, Laverne Brickhouse.*

Club for thirty-eight years, was looked up to by many as the granddaddy of all the hunting clubs around here after Mr. John Poyner died. Mr. Poyner had been superintendent of Currituck Shooting Club from 1909 until he retired in 1960.

Mr. Carl knew Mr. Earl Slick. He and Mr. Orville Woodhouse had sold Mr. Slick the Narrows Island property. Mr. Carl and Mr. Woodhouse got a little hustle out of that. Mr. Woodhouse had been leasing Narrows Island from P.K. Gravely and other owners of the China American Tobacco Company in Rocky Mount, North Carolina, and he knew them. Mr. Slick had hunted at Pine Island, and Mr. Carl knew him and got in touch with him. Mr. Slick bought the Pine Island property in the fall of 1972. This was five miles from sound to ocean from Caffey's Inlet to the Currituck Club Line, except for eight hundred feet at Caffey's Inlet from sound to ocean that Mr. Carl White owned. This was about four miles in Currituck County and one mile in Dare County.

Remember, Walter Davis had bought six hundred acres of oceanfront from Currituck Shooting Club, which he later sold to James Johnson after the first Whalehead and Pine Island deals fell through. He made the development of Ocean Sands. The plan was approved for Ocean Sands in 1973, and development was started.

The Road

I really hate to start this. I would like to just skirt it, but I talked to Susan Davis, who wrote *The Whalehead Club: Reflections of Currituck Heritage* and is the person completely responsible for me writing my first book. I told her I just hate to get into this road. She said, "You can't do that. I did that in my book. You've got to tell about it."

There could be a whole book written about that road.

Mama kept everything that was written about Currituck beach. I'm going to try to hit the highlights of what I know myself, and after giving it some thought, I feel like I'm going to have to include right much from the scrapbooks. If Mama thought it was important enough to cut it out of a paper or magazine and put it in her scrapbook, I decided I should make myself put it in my book at least as a reference for future generations to use.

They had been going back and forth about a road to Corolla about as long as they had about the bridge to Corolla. I'm not going to begin to get into all that, but I am going to include a lot of it.

In 1971, Bob Scott was governor of North Carolina. The Highway Commission was surveying a right of way for a seventeen-mile road from Duck to Corolla. The county commissioners wanted a road built so the beach could develop and they could collect more tax revenue.

I saw them surveying, saw the stakes, so I figured it was going to happen.

ROAD TO COROLLA TO BENEFIT FEW

Pat Stith (October 1971)

(From Mama's Scrapbook)

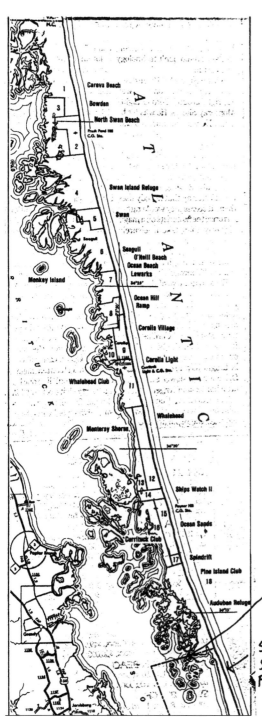

The State of North Carolina declined for environmental reasons to provide access to Bald Head Island, but it seems to be moving towards construction of a development highway through one of the last unspoiled beaches on the Outer Banks

Next month the Highway Commission will finish surveying the right of way for a 17-mile highway from Duck to Corolla, along a virtually uninhabited Currituck County beach.

That road would please the Currituck Commissioners who want a road built and the beach developed so they can increase the county tax revenue. It would give 17 people who live in Corolla easier access to the outside world…an access some of them do not want.

Map showing developments on Currituck Beach. I've had this map a long time and can't remember where it came from. It is either a county or state map. *Author's collection.*

68

Corolla Access

Sept. 1982

GUARDHOUSE GANG — Members of the N.C. Board of Transportation toured the Currituck Banks last week to inspect the private road which the Department of Transportation has considered acquiring as a public thoroughfare. Environmental hearing followed in Currituck High School, but all that seemed to have resulted was placing the DOT in the middle of the squabble over development of the Outer Banks. If the road becomes public, Dot will be accused of opening the Banks to a rush of real estate development. If the road remains private, board will be charged with denying rights of access to Corolla natives, etc,. etc., etc. Among those present at the Ocean Sands guardhouse are, more or less left-to-right. DOT Secretary William Roberson, Manteo Board Member Marc Basnight, County Manager Walton Carter, in center, and on right Commissioner Baxter Williams eclipsing Planning Board Chairman Travis Morris.
Post Photo by Mason Peters

Corolla Access, "Guardhouse Gang." Photo is by Mason Peters and from September 1982. *Courtesy Mama's scrapbook.*

Finally it would enrich the three property owners who control more than two-thirds of the beach front through which the road is being surveyed.

All this would cost the state $1.7 million, not counting the cost of acquiring the right of way.

Corolla is accessible only by boat or by four wheel drive vehicle and area Highway Commissioner Joe W. Nowell, Jr. told the News & Observer, *"I think we owe these people an access in and out."*

First Division Engineer D.W. Patrick, who made the $1.7 million cost estimate, said the cost estimate is being made at the request of the Currituck

County Commissioners, that the commissioners, want "an all-weather means of ingress and egress" from Corolla "to the so-called outside world."

"That would be the main reason that this project was rejuvenated," Patrick said.

ONLY THREE CHILDREN

Their spokesman, William Brumsey, III, argued for the road on behalf of the school children of Corolla. Because the village is isolated, Brumsey said, the children must live away from home so they can attend school.

Brumsey did not say only three children were in that predicament. Nor did he tell the father of these children, or the Highway Commission, that Gene O. Austin, 37, is neutral about the road.

"In a way I hate to see it and in away I don't," Austin told a reporter. "Being isolated like it is really is the beauty of it."

THE PEOPLE'S FORUM

Corolla Resident Backs Road to Corolla

(From Mama's Scrapbook)

To the Editor: Your story "Corolla Road to Benefit Few" that appeared in the Sunday edition, October 17th, by Pat Stith, was a story well done I feel sure. If he were to write fiction novels I know he would become a well-known author.

However, in all fairness to the people who live here and pay taxes to the County of Currituck and the state of North Carolina and receive nothing in return, and the children who are denied access for an education it prompts me to make a reply to such a story. For instance, when did Gene Austin become the only one who has children that such a road would benefit and indicated that this road is not wanted by this family, when it is a matter of public record that Mr. and Mrs. Austin along with other parents, visited the Currituck County Board of Commissioners and Board of Education in the fall of 1969, protesting the schooling situation as it exists here.

When it comes to denying children an access to and from a school I can't agree with your writer that such a road would benefit few. This year there is one child living along this route who is carried to Dare County each morning by his parents and placed on a bus to attend school in Kitty Hawk; three children are boarded away from home on the Currituck County mainland; three other children attend school in Chesapeake, Virginia, and are carried back and forth daily by their parents; four children ride the Virginia Beach school bus that comes to the North Carolina line to attend school in Virginia Beach. There are 29 other children of school age whose parents live elsewhere because there is no school or transportation is provided, while paying taxes to the County of Currituck and state of North Carolina.

It seems strange that Mr. Stith didn't interview for his story the many families who own homes here but have had to move away because nothing is done towards the progress of the community or that he didn't interview the families living here who are in favor of a road.

As for traffic volume a recent news release by the Department of Interior on traffic studies made to determine the number of vehicles using the beach here indicates that from 3 to 6000 cars use the beach daily during the summer months, a volume that I doubt many of our small western part of the state towns have and roads seem to be built up there without regard to benefits, with my tax money.

John W. Austin

Mr. Austin—"Been here ever since." *Courtesy Mama's scrapbook.*

71

COROLLA

December 1971

(From Mama's Scrapbook)

A shaft of sunlight outlined the valleys and hills in the worn grain of the Post Office floor as John Austin talked of the prosperity his village had known.

Austin, like other residents of the wind-buffeted Carolina coast, a thin sliver of sand and grass between the Atlantic and Currituck Sound, awaits a Department of the Interior decision that may affect his life and dreams.

The decision, expected early next month, will restrict vehicular traffic on the Back Bay Wildlife Refuge beach to "substantial property owners," according to a refuge official. The shoreline is the only link between Carolina and Virginia Beach.

The refuge policy change was prompted by thousands of vehicles, many ill equipped, which descend on the beach any summer weekend, scarring the shoreline with tire tracks, beer cans and litter.

In addition to the esthetic blemishes wrought by the inconsiderate, conservationists believe the traffic effects the wildlife population and causes dune erosion…

Mr. Johnny made his first trip to Virginia Beach in 1907. "It was just three fish camps, a bar and a dancehall then," he said. The first trip was made in a paddlewheel steamer, subsequent trips along the beach by horse.

Austin remembers a Virginia Beach of grocery stores with hitching posts and streets ankle deep in mud… "Now look at the place."

He feels that progress would have come to Corolla "long ago, if we had a road down here. The young people leave because there is no work for them."

Whatever the ruling, Austin will stay. "I left Corolla several times; saw England, France, Italy during and after World War I…even spent some time on the Riviera."

"I had a good job in Washington too, but every year I looked up and saw the geese returning to Currituck Sound. I wanted to come back; so I did," he explained.

"I've never regretted it," he added, looking around the small post office/ snack stand, "a satisfied mind is worth everything."

Les Thornbury, Ben Taylor, Jerry Hardesty and Stewart Udall discuss development
Courtesy Mama's scrapbook.

VIRGINIAN PILOT:
UDALL INSPECTS CURRITUCK BANKS

Frank Roberts (April 29, 1972)

(From Mama's Scrapbook)

CURRITUCK—Former Interior Secretary Stewart Udall roamed Currituck County's Outer banks Friday, then called for state officials to help plan future development there…

A cabinet officer in the Kennedy and Johnson Administration, Udall said the state should be asked to create and fund a planning agency to work with local and federal officials to plan area development.

Udall, now chairman of Overview, Incorporated, a Washington organization devoted to community planning, said the banks could best be developed in clustered areas surrounded by open, undeveloped areas…

Udall's tour was conducted by Currituck Planning Board Chairman Jerry Hardesty, Les Thornbury, one of the student group organizers; and

Ben Taylor, a Currituck native and president of Envirotek Company, a Raleigh concern that Taylor said, "reconciles development with the environment."

VIRGINIAN PILOT: CURRITUCK STOPS NEW PROJECTS ON OUTER BANKS

Frank Roberts (May 2, 1972)

(From Mama's Scrapbook)

Currituck County Commissioners Monday placed a temporary moratorium on the Outer Banks, agreed to request each development that has already begun work to consecrate on a single area, and appropriated $5,000 toward a development plan for the banks.

The temporary moratorium will last six to eight months, while the county prepares a development plan for the 23 mile stretch between Duck and the Virginia line.

VIRGINIAN PILOT: SUPPORT FOLLOWS PLEAS FOR PLANNED DEVELOPMENT

Frank Roberts (1972)

(From Mama's Scrapbook)

Raleigh—After a plea was made by seven North Carolina State University students and former Interior Secretary Stewart Udall to develop Currituck County's Outer Banks without destroying its environment, offers of financial and political support were made to the county…

Three major Currituck County developers, Jim Kabler, O.J. Frink, and Earl Slick, indicated strongly they will work toward proper development of the 23 mile stretch between Duck and the Virginia line, the longest undeveloped coastal area in the Eastern United States…

Bryan Sigman (student) also suggested that the village of Corolla, "be preserved for history."

Governor Bob Scott ponders plan. *Courtesy Mama's scrapbook.*

"Since Currituck County's Outer Banks are virtually undeveloped,"
Sigman said, "you can avoid mistakes made elsewhere."

SCOTT PROMISES TO
BACK CURRITUCK DEVELOPMENT

May 26, 1972

(From Mama's Scrapbook)

Governor Bob Scott gave his personal endorsement to a plan for orderly development of the Currituck Outer Banks.

The area is the longest stretch of the undeveloped beach along the East Coast.

Jerry Hardesty, chairman of the county planning board; H.D. Newbern, commission chairman; and Nathan Roberts, commissioner, discussed the development plans with the governor in his office for a half hour.

Scott said the initiative shown by Currituck officials "is nothing short of amazing. It's unheard of in this state."

The governor said he has always been interested in long-range planning, "This fits right into my concept."

He suggested that a task force of state officials be organized to assure state assistance; but emphasized the main thrust should come from the county.

"The implications are statewide," he said, "but I'm a strong believer in local government."

"Your actions," he told Currituck officials, "will show other counties how it can be done."

The proposal the officials brought to the governor cited suitable road access for the area as top priority, as well as environmental protection before, during, and after development of the beach.

Presently the only access is by four-wheel drive vehicle or by boat.

In a March 21, 1973 newspaper article written by Daniel C. Hoover he said the State Highway Commission had formerly abandoned any plans for building a road from Duck to Corolla.

The same article says the proposals for the road date back to the 1930s, when the state agreed to accept the road if the old Works Progress Administration (WPA) would build it. The WPA never built the road, but the phantom road has been on the map ever since.

The channel going into the boat basin at Corolla was kept open by Gene Austin and me, going in and out of there with our gas boats (inboard motorboats). Mr. J.I. Hayman and others also went in there to go fishing on the beach.

Now, those that have power over maintaining a channel say there was never a channel there. If that be the case, why has the Coast Guard maintained two beacons leading into the boat basin at the Whalehead Club since the 1940s? They still maintain them. One is right at the end of the airstrip. When you got to that beacon, you headed for the west chimney of the Whalehead Club. There was a port and starboard light on each side of the chimney until Brindley got the place.

S.E. Caroon from Waterlily had a little dredge. I got the county commissioners to agree to pay for getting a channel fifty feet wide and six feet deep from the inside beacon at the end of the airstrip to the humpback bridge at the mouth of the boat basin. He was also going to dredge about an acre basin out in front of the county dock.

I got Elmo Williams, a surveyor from Elizabeth City, to come over here, and I took him in my boat. He surveyed it and staked it out with white PVC pipe. The dredging was going to cost $4,000, and we were going to put the spoil on the airstrip. Some young woman who worked in an office at the courthouse had connections through her brother with the Corp of Engineers, and she was going to take care of getting the permit. Things were not tight as they are now. This was, I think, in late 1972.

In 1973, James E. Holshouser Jr., a Republican, took over as governor and that ended the road to Corolla.

Now Kabler & Riggs told the North Carolina Highway Commission they would give $1 million toward a ferry from Waterlily to Corolla. This was being considered. I told them they could buy the farm at the south end of Waterlily, which was around fifty acres, for $50,000. It was owned by Dodson Mathias at the time. I marked a shoving pole in feet and took three men— Jimmy Lee, assistant head of Bridge Maintenance and Engine Operations; Marine Engineer Ray Dossett, who was a state of North Carolina highway administrator; and Graham Pervier, county manager—in my gas boat *Rhonda* and showed them at the south end of Waterlily how far they'd have to dredge, which was not very far, to get to four feet of water. Then, we went across the sound, and I showed them how far they'd have to dredge from the outside beacon to the inside beacon at the end of the airstrip to have four feet of water. That was not too far either. We went on in the boat basin, and they laid a plan of the ferry out on the engine box of my boat. They had the name "Corolla" on the drawing of the ferry.

I told the county commissioners that if the state was going to dredge for a ferry there was no need to get S.E. Caroon to dredge out the channel. Long story short, the ferry didn't happen. They said it would cost too much to maintain it. Many a time since, I've wished we'd gotten that channel dredged out when we could. So much for the channel.

CURRITUCK APPROVES OCEAN FRONT PROJECT

Bill Baumann (May 9 1973)

(From Mama's Scrapbook)

Negotiations have been concluded between the Currituck County Commissioners and Coastland Corporation of Virginia Beach, Virginia, for a 250 acre, ocean front tract on the Outer Banks, five miles north of the Dare County line.

Coastland, which has dubbed the property, "Ocean Sands" intends to construct both single family and condominium housing units using the "cluster" concept, at an approximate cost of $20 million. Ultimately about 3,600 units are planned. Under terms of the firm's agreement with Currituck, the county will design, engineer, construct and operate both sewage treatment and water supply facilities for the development. It is estimated the plants will cost about $560,000.

In return the county will be paid $2,800 per developable acre within Ocean Sands. Additionally, Coastland will provide all lateral sewage and water connections within the subdivision.

The agreement put Currituck in the central sewer and water business for the first time in the coastal county's history. Because of the precedent setting move, county commissioners studied the contract at length before giving it their final approval.

Termed a "forward step in protecting the environment" by representatives of Coastland the development will leave a minimum of 30 percent of the property undeveloped.

Plans for Ocean Sands were approved by the North Carolina Department of Natural and Economic Resources and the North Carolina Department of Public Health.

Moor Gardner and Assoc., Inc., a Greensboro engineering firm, hired by Currituck County, also studied and approved Coastland's plans.

Access to the development will be by means of an easement through Earl Slick's property through Ocean Sands. Slick, of Winston Salem, owns around 800 acres on the Outer Banks.

Under terms of the agreement between Slick and Coastland a private sand or clay road will be constructed from the Dare County line to Ocean Sands. Only permanent residents owning property north of Ocean Sands, property owners in the development and their guests will be permitted past the security guard at the road's head.

Coastland has agreed to fence the road at Slick's discretion. Should a causeway ever be constructed across Currituck Sound in the Corolla vicinity, the easement will be terminated.

Although Coastland Corporation headed by James Johnson, Jr., of Virginia Beach, is now planning to develop 250 acres, the firm owns 635 acres on the Outer Banks. Estimates of the lands tax value are running from $100 million to $140 million after Ocean Sands is completed.

DAILY ADVANCE PROTECTION OF CURRITUCK OUTER BANKS IS ENDORSED

Bill Baumann (Thursday, June 28, 1973)

(From Mama's Scrapbook)

Poplar Branch—Carefully planned development and protection of Currituck County's Virgin Outer Banks is recommended by the Currituck Plan, a portion of which was introduced here last night at a public hearing.

Assembled through the corporation of numerous state and local agencies as well as private consultants, the plan makes specific recommendations for access, building construction, water and sewage treatment, environmental protection and creation of a new state park at Monkey Island.

The Currituck Outer Banks is one of the "unique natural areas on the East Coast", according to the plan's authors. Relatively untouched by mankind, the 23-mile-long, windswept strand is presentably accessible by boat and four-wheel drive vehicle.

Because of the area's close proximity to metropolitan Norfolk's one million residents, county commissioners agreed in 1972 to prepare for its inevitable development. The resulting Currituck Plan was written through a team approach employing personnel from N.C. State University, the U.S. Soil Conservation Service, State Department of Transportation, Department of Natural and Economic Resources, and other state and federal agencies.

Numerous private individuals and firms also contributed to the report.

The bulk of the plan funding came from private sources. Jim Shaw of Coastal Plains Regional Commission announced last night that a $35,000 grant had been approved by Governor Jim Holshouser to complete the study of Currituck County.

The Outer Banks development plans were influenced by a number of factors. Physical characteristics—soil types, wildlife habits, shifting dune and wash over zones, scenic locales, water tables and flood areas—all shape the final proposal.

Land values, taxes, proximity to populated areas, recreational potential and the owner's plan for his land were also considered by authors of the Currituck Plan.

Access to the Currituck Outer Banks has been cited by Ben Taylor of Envirotek Inc., prime planning consultants for the county, as a crucial element in the area's development.

Construction of a thoroughfare North–South highway down the sandy beach from the Virginia line to US 158 in Kitty Hawk is not recommended by the planners. Instead, they propose that two separate "destination beaches" rather than one "thoroughfare beach" be created. This unique approach envisions ferry connections between the Outer Banks in Currituck in two locations for "cultural and economic reasons."

These ferries would service two separate developable areas on Currituck Outer Banks. The southern boats operate from either Aydlett or Waterlily and a point just south of Corolla. The Knotts Island ferry is proposed to continue to the Carova Beach area.

Sources indicate that when ferry service in these two locations is implemented Coastland's easement through Slicks property will be terminated. This action would effectively stop traffic between Ocean Sands and the Dare County line.

Lots measuring 6,000 square feet in the development, on the Atlantic, will be sold for about $33,000 according to Johnson. Construction on the access road will begin immediately.

MEETING WITH EARL SLICK

Now, James Johnson and Kabler & Riggs needed a road for the developments of Ocean Sands and Whalehead. They got a meeting arranged with Mr. Slick to see about getting a right of way to build a private road through his property.

At this time, Kabler & Riggs's agents were driving the beach from their office in Sandbridge, Virginia, to sell the Whalehead property. Back Bay Wildlife Refuge had not closed off driving the beach through the refuge at this time.

Bill Hollan, Mr. Slick's right-hand man, told me that Gardner was in the meeting and said that Kabler & Riggs could have had the same deal Johnson had if Sam Riggs hadn't have flown hot and walked out of the meeting. Riggs said a few words I can't print here and said he didn't need the right of way; he'd drive down the beach. Mr. Slick told Riggs he'd be back.

Johnson made a deal with Mr. Slick and paved a right of way through the Pine Island property and put up a gate and guardhouse. He wouldn't let anybody through except his property owners who were buying land in his development, Ocean Sands. This was the Walter Davis land.

If you wonder why the road through the Pine Island property has so many curves in it, I'll tell you what Mr. Carl White told me and Bill Hollan verified. Mr. Slick didn't want a straight road because people would be racing up and down through there. Mr. Carl told me he got on a bulldozer with the operator and curved out around places like Sue's Cabin and places like that where he thought the road might bother the ducks.

Folks, I'm trying my best to keep these stories in sequence, but I'm having a time with it. As soon as I think I'm through with the road, I'll see something else in a scrapbook I just don't feel like I can leave out. Just now I called Susan Davis and told her I don't know how in the world I let her talk me into getting into all this road doings. Another thing is what you read in these newspapers is not always exactly like it is. I'm hesitant to talk to reporters because I never know how it's going to come out in the paper. It's not that reporters are trying to tell something wrong. They just don't thoroughly understand what they are talking about sometimes.

Here's another story I just ran across.

DEVELOPERS ARE DISPUTING OVER NORTH–SOUTH HIGHWAY.

Bill Baumann (September 9, 1973)

(From Mama's Scrapbook)

Currituck—Efforts by county commissioners to prevent the construction of a public north–south highway on Currituck's Outer Banks may be the cause of a dispute between two coastal area developers, the Daily Advance *has learned.*

Sam Riggs of Kabler & Riggs Realtors stated Friday that Coastland Corporation of Virginia Beach had been given permission by Currituck commissioners to build a private road through the firm's 550 acre Ocean Sands development which lies about four miles north of the Dare County line on the Atlantic Ocean.

All other Outer Banks Developers, including Kabler & Riggs, were required to submit plats to the commissioners which provide for a public thoroughfare, Riggs said.

A check with the Register of Deeds office revealed that Coastland's plat specifies "all streets and access easements are reserved by the owner, its successors or assigns as private roads." The main north–south street through Ocean Sands, "Ocean Trail," is marked as private on that plat.

Publicity and sales literature released by Coastland emphasizes that only property owners and their guests will be permitted to enter the development. "Access to Ocean Sands will be over a private road…privacy will be assured through 24 hour security at the entrance," one company news release claims.

However, Jerry Hardesty, Chairman of the Currituck County Planning Board, denies that permission has been given Coastland permission for a private road.

"The Board of Commissioners never said, in the end analysis, to my knowledge, that there will be a private road," Hardesty said.

He added that Article Eight, Section One of the Currituck County Subdivisions Regulations requires that "every lot shall front or abut on a public street or shall front on an all-weather access to a public drive."

Hardesty said that while the commissioners "don't have any intention of favoring Johnson (President of Coastland Corporation) over Kabler & Riggs," they may have approved the Ocean Sands plat in hopes of preventing construction of a public north–south highway on the banks.

The Currituck Plan, a comprehensive study of the county by Federal, state and local agencies as well as several private consulting firms, recommends that access to the Outer Banks be limited to two ferries. The boats would service two "destination" beaches, separated by a state park at Corolla.

The plan, which has been approved by Currituck Commissioners, warns against a "thoroughfare beach" which would be created, according to the authors, if a continuous highway was built from the Dare County line at Duck north along the banks.

The state has been slow to provide funds for the ferries, Hardesty said. "This never would have happened if the state would have done what they said they would," he told the Advance. *"They've got us over a barrel." Hardesty added.*

Gary Cowan, executive vice-president of Coastland, said he is confident that his firm owns the only private access to the Outer Banks. "The plats have been approved by the county commissioners," Cowan added.

His firm obtained an easement through Earl Slick's property which lies between Coastland's tract and the Dare County line to the south. The 3.8 mile sand and clay road will be constructed at an approximate cost of $300,000, sources indicate.

Earlier this week, the Advance *reported an alleged offer made to Kabler & Riggs by Coastland for use of the road which could be the sole means of* access from the south to Kabler's 1,500 acre Whalehead land development if ferry service is not initiated. Whalehead encompasses the Corolla area and borders Ocean Sands on the north.

When Currituck's commissioners heard of the alleged bargain, which was labeled both a "hard bargain" and "extortion" by two board members, a request for approval of Coastland's Phase III was tabled.

Cowan denied that any offer was made to Kabler & Riggs adding that, "We are not considering talking to them in the future."

Hardesty and Currituck's fledgling County Manager, Graham Pervier, were in Raleigh Friday discussing the access problem and related issues with the county's engineers as well as representatives from Envirotek, consultants to the county plan.

Hardesty stated that county officials would "continue to push hard for an east–west access to the banks." Meanwhile a meeting with representatives from Kabler & Riggs, Coastland Corporation and county officials is scheduled for early next week.

DAILY ADVANCE FINAL ACTION IS POSTPONED ON CURRITUCK LAND PROJECT

Bill Baumann (*September 14, 1973*)

(From Mama's Scrapbook)

Currituck—County commissioners unanimously voted to "defer action" on Coastland Corporation's Phase III plats last night pending "clarification of the question of access."

Decision came after a sometimes noisy meeting of principles in the dispute which "left a bad taste in my mouth," according to Coastland Executive Vice-President Gary Cowan.

The controversy centers around a private right-of-way agreement made between the Currituck County Commissioners and Coastland Corporation earlier this year. Coastland is developing a 550 acre tract, Ocean Sands, which lies about four miles north of the Dare County line.

Plats for one phase of the project specify that the main north–south road, "Ocean Trail," will be private. The plats were approved by the commissioners.

Because access to the Outer Banks from the north has been cut off by federal court order, the southern route through Ocean Sands has become of serious concern to Kabler & Riggs, developers of North Swan Beach, Swan Beach, Corova Beach, and Whalehead.

Kabler, Riggs, Cowan and several other Outer Banks land owners as well as attorneys representing the principles were at last night's meeting.

County Manager Graham Pervier opened the meeting by stating that he felt it was an unfortunate oversight that Ocean Trail was platted as a private road.

"However," he continued, "I think it's important that the main thoroughfare be a public street for our vehicles (county garbage trucks, utility vehicles etc.)"

Coastland's Cowan then replied, "You must remember you have told us the road will be private and we have passed that information on to our property owners. We will be liable to millions of dollars in lawsuits if that road is made public."

"Someone has to be liable for those damages," Cowan warned.

Publicity and sales literature released by the firm emphasizes that only property owners and their guests will be permitted to enter the development. "Access to Ocean Sands will be over a private road…Privacy will be assured through 24-hour security at the entrance," one company brochure promises.

Kenyon Wilson, representing Kabler & Riggs as well as "4,000 property owners on the Outer Banks" then told the commissioners, "It's a foregone conclusion that the (northern access) is out. You've got a responsibility to remember those people up north."

"If these gentlemen (Coastland's representatives) want to cooperate let them make a public access until such time as an east–west access is put through."

Wilson's reference was to a proposed ferry system which is envisioned in the Currituck Plan. The boats would service two "destination beaches" and would "hopefully prevent a U.S. 158 business-bypass situation such as the one existing in Dare County," according to Pervier.

To Wilson's suggestion that Coastland make the road through their property public, Cowan snapped, "I don't think that you understand that we have no option open to us. Our hands are tied."

"I don't see how there can be any misunderstanding as long as the plats are recorded in this courthouse," he stated.

Pervier then proposed that a temporary bypass be built around Coastland's private road through Currituck Shooting Club until the proposed ferry system can be implemented by the state.

Wilson said, "Knowing the Currituck Club as I do, I really don't hold any hope for an easement."

Pervier then recommended that the commissioners approve the Coastland plat while stipulating that they would be "reluctant" to approve further plats until a temporary north–south easement arrangement is worked out by Coastland and Kabler & Riggs.

Wilson warned that such a decision by the commissioners would "leave 4,000 people totally stranded." Presently access to Corolla and developments to the north is only possible with four-wheel drive vehicle and boats across Currituck Sound.

Commissioner Marvin Snowden then moved that no further action be taken on the Coastland Plats until the developers could work out an amiable access plan. Cowan stated that, "we have been out of business for three months with no inventory (land tracts) to sell while we were redesigning Ocean Sands in accordance with the Currituck Plan."

"I repeat that postponing action on this plat (Phase II) of Ocean Sands is a very significant step and tremendously unfair."

"I don't think we've concluded this meeting in a spirit of good faith," he added before leaving.

A letter recently received by Currituck commissioner H.D. Newbern from Assistant Secretary of Transportation John Cameron indicates that "an analysis of the difficult access problems of the Currituck Outer Banks is now an active transportation planning project."

"We anticipate our recommendations will reach the Secretary of Transportation by December 1," Cameron wrote.

DAILY ADVANCE COMMITTED FUNDING MAY SCUTTLE FERRY OPERATION

Bill Baumann (December 20, 1973)

(From Mama's Scrapbook)

Currituck—The state-funded ferry operation envisioned in the Currituck Plan may be scuttled by a financially hard-pressed Department of Transportation, Assistant Secretary John Cameron told county commissioners Wednesday.

"All the department's funding is committed under our seven year construction plan," Cameron said. He cautioned, however, that his fact

finding visit to the Currituck Banks was not intended to "Make any decisions or bring tidings of great joy."

Cameron's boss, Bruce Lentz, has promised a decision on the two proposed Outer Banks ferries, which would shuttle between Corolla and Waterlily and Knotts Island and the Carova Beach area, by the first of the year.....

Al Grizette, a staff planner who accompanied Cameron, said the going rate for a ferry is $500,000 while the boats would cost $200,000 annually to operate.

Citing the limited public facilities on the outer banks Cameron stated "At this point and time I find it very hard to understand why I as a taxpayer should pay for access for these private developments."

Cameron suggested, however, that private developers on the banks may be willing to purchase and operate the ferry despite its high cost...

"I know your planners have sold you on a destination beach," Cameron said, adding, "I hasten to remind you that you have a destination beach with the north blocked off."

The secretary's reference was to the alternate southern access route through Earl Slick's property which lies just north of the Dare County line.

Coastland Corporation of Virginia Beach has secured a right-of-way through Slick's land and Kabler & Riggs, also of Virginia Beach, have been told they too could purchase access through Slick's track if Currituck Commissioners approve their planned unit development.

Construction of a road from the Dare line to the southern-most development on the Currituck Banks would be equally as expensive as a ferry, Cameron said. "It's six in one, half a dozen in the other," he stated.

The commissioners then passed a resolution affirming their belief that ferry access would be more satisfactory than a north–south highway.

DAILY ADVANCE TRANSPORTATION SECRETARY ENDORSES FERRY SERVICE

Bill Bauman (February 1974)

(From Mama's Scrapbook)

Currituck—State Secretary of Transportation Bruce Lentz met personally with county officials here Monday and endorsed the development of a passenger-oriented east–west ferry service to the Currituck Outer Banks and a non automobile transit system for internal circulation on the new-virgin strip of beach…

Three representatives of the Clark-Frates Corporation, a Dallas-based land development firm attended the meeting last night.

The Daily Advance *learned from one of the Clark-Frates team that the corporation has obtained a 60 day option to purchase the Monkey Island tract near Corolla on the Banks.*

One source indicated the price for the land may exceed $3 million. A reliable source also predicted a portion of the property may yet be obtained by the state for use as a state park. The Currituck Plan envisions a state park in the Monkey Island area which will include the village of Corolla.

TRANSPORTATION OFFICIALS INVESTIGATE FERRY SITES

Leo Boatwright

(From Mama's Scrapbook; no date or source)

Currituck—Officials from the North Carolina Department of Transportation spent Thursday afternoon here taking a "detailed look" at potential sites for the county's second ferry service linking the mainland with the Outer Banks…

"We want to help the people of Currituck and the people of the state," said Al Grisette, transportation planner for the N.C. Department of Transportation. "Once the access issue is resolved we hope to initiate the service as soon as possible."

Jimmy Lee, assistant head of Bridge Maintenance and Engine Operations and Marine Engineer Ray Dossett were on hand as Pervier and Travis Morris of Currituck Realty Co. conducted the tour of the sound between Waterlily and Corolla…

The state and area developers plan to unite to pay for the service across the five mile track.

$1 MILLION OFFER REFUSED BY TRANSPORTATION AGENCY

July 18, 1974

(From Mama's Scrapbook; no other references given)

The $1 million offer made by Outer Banks developers to the North Carolina Department of Transportation for establishment of a ferry service has been turned down.

Transportation Secretary Troy Doby said Wednesday the offer did not provide sufficient funds to plan the ferry but the rejection did not mean the state is against the ferry. "It's just this particular offer," he said

The offer was made by Kabler & Riggs Realtors of Virginia Beach, Va. and a Texas firm…

Riggs has reported that he and Kabler may develop another southern access road to their property but have made no plans for an access from the north.

There are so many articles on this issue that I could fill the book, but my publisher will only allow so many words.

I got along with Kabler & Riggs mainly because of my friendship with Gerald Friedman. I used the Whalehead Club boat basin to come into from Waterlily. I didn't sell land for the realty group because they only wanted to pay me 3 percent commission.

I did sell a few lots for James Johnson, and he did pay me 10 percent and let me have a pass to get through the gate.

When U.S. Fish & Wildlife cut off access through the Back Bay Refuge, which put a halt to Kabler & Riggs's sales of the Whalehead property, the partners were forced to deal with Mr.

Back Bay National Wildlife Refuge. *Author's collection.*

"Berlin Wall," as we call it, is the barbed wire fence between Carova Beach and Back Bay Wildlife Refuge. This is also the North Carolina–Virginia line. *Author's collection.*

Slick. If I remember right, they had to pay Mr. Slick $800,000, of which Johnson got $300,000.

Shortly after they had paid him the money, I was riding with Jim Kabler and Sam Riggs for some reason up that road. We got to the gate and the guard wouldn't let us through. Sam Riggs's face got as red as a beet, and I thought he was going to have a stroke. No such thing as cellphones then. They had a phone in the guardhouse. After many words that can't be printed here, he finally got Johnson on the phone, and we got through the gate.

It is rumored that James Johnson owed Walter Davis money, and he was in default. One day, Walter Davis and his boat captain, Charlie Midgett, were riding out and decided to ride up Currituck Beach. When they got to the gate, the guard wouldn't let them through. Davis didn't say anything. He got out of his car and went around to the back, opened the trunk and took out an assault rifle. He didn't make any threats or say a word, just held the rifle. The guard had a change of mind and let them through. It seems Davis carried the rifle when his old enemy Dr. Armand Hammer was looking to harm him. He never needed the gun for safety, but he kept it handy.

Now, as a real estate agent, I had a pass to get through the gate. My wife and I owned several pieces of property in Corolla Village. The only way she or my children could go through the gate was with me.

The people I had sold to in Corolla Village couldn't get a pass to go through the gate. I think it was in 1971 that Kenyon Wilson, Cyrus Aydlett, Don Rochon and I bought one hundred acres up around Penny Hill. Part of it was north of the hill, and the rest of it was south of the hill. We started a development called Sea Gull, now Penny Hill by the Sea. I had sold one lot when Johnson put up the gate. I stopped selling lots there. I was not going to knowingly sell property to people who couldn't get to their property, not even with four-wheel drive.

Now, I had a problem. Remember Mr. Carl White was one of the owners of Corolla Village, and he was still superintendent of Pine Island Club after Mr. Slick bought it; he was also superintendent of Narrows Island Club, which Mr. Slick owned.

Up to this point, I had never met Mr. Slick. I asked Mr. Carl to introduce me to him. At the appointed day and time, I went to Pine Island Club. I had never been there before. Mr. Carl met me at the front door and took me to the west room of the clubhouse. This room had been added on to the living room. It had a lot of windows overlooking the yard, which in the wintertime was always full of ducks. They called it Potter's Room. I've heard it had something to do with a poker game. That's hearsay; I don't know.

Mr. Carl introduced me to Mr. Slick, and his attorney, Paul Mickey. I can't remember if Bill Hollan was there or not.

After the introductions, I gave Mr. Slick the original deed when Mr. Barney bought the property. My daddy had represented Mr. Barney when he bought the property in 1935. Of course, it had been recorded, but the original had been in Daddy's safe ever since 1935. It was just a keepsake, but I thought it might give me a little credibility.

I told Mr. Slick my problem and told him that when he let James Johnson have that easement over his property I didn't think that he meant for Johnson to have a hammer over everybody else's head that had property up the beach. He said, "No, I certainly didn't." He looked at Paul Mickey and said, "Paul, I can let who I want to go up there can't I?" Paul Mickey after a long silence finally said, "No, I don't think so." That was the first time Mr. Slick knew he couldn't let who he wanted to go through the property. I heard that Paul Mickey had let Johnson's attorney write the agreement, and he hadn't looked over it too well. It was easy to see Mr. Slick was upset.

At the time, Mr. Carl White owned eight hundred feet from sound to ocean where the Caffey's Inlet Coast Guard station was (now the Sanderlin Inn and Restaurant).

Mr. Slick looked at Mr. Carl and said, "Carl you still own that eight hundred feet up there; we'll put him on his knees and make him jump crack backs."

As it turns out, the state had been grading the road that far up there, and there was nothing they could do about it.

Mr. Slick did intercede for me with James Johnson. When my office burned in 1980, there were just a few files that were packed so tight in a drawer in my desk that they burned around the edges, but you could still read them.

I'm going to copy this letter for you verbatim:

May 11, 1977

Mr. Travis Morris
Currituck Realty
Post Office Drawer 66
Coinjock, North Carolina 27923

Dear Travis:

This is to acknowledge receipt of monies for Corolla Village.

To re-state our understanding as discussed on the telephone the other day it is as follows: Coastland Corporation will permit you to be the "clearinghouse" for the individual property owners in Corolla Village who will be granted access on an individual lot basis. The charges will be a non-refundable $250 charge plus $125 per year charge for the pass.

If this does not meet with your complete understanding, please advise me.

Enclosed you will find the pass permit for Mr. John Lawrence Hyde of Phoenix, Maryland, owner of lot 40, section 3, Corolla Village.

Very truly yours,
OCEAN SANDS, INC.
James
James E. Johnson, Jr.
President

I thought this was reasonable. We couldn't expect to ride the paved road for nothing.

COURT CASE

On September 19, 1975, Judge Herbert Small granted a temporary restraining order that would stop Earl Slick and James Johnson from blocking access to ten property owners in the Corolla area from crossing their property to get to Corolla.

SEPTEMBER 19, 1975

(From Mama's Scrapbook)

The order was issued this morning in Elizabeth City. It will remain in effect until September 29 when respondents are to appear in Currituck County Superior Court at 10:00 a.m.

The order concerns the use of Secondary Road 1152 from the Currituck-Dare line to Poyner's Hill.

The order states that section of road "appears to be public road, no longer maintained by the Department of Transportation and "'abandoned' thereby, and hence a public road."

Plaintiffs in the order are Margart M. West, Clifford Scott, Caleb Poyner, Elwyn Walker, James O. Dunton, Phyllis Adams Arey, Donald Adams, Samuel H. Lamb, Samuel H. Lamb II and Pamela V. Weiland.

Defendants named are Earl F. Slick, and wife, Jane P. Slick; Pine Island Development Venture; RDC, Inc.; Clark Frates Corp.; Joseph A. Frates and wife, Johanna I. Frates; Rex D. Frates and wife, Marianne Frates; James E. Johnson Jr.; and Coastland Corp.

To summarize an October 15, 1975 article, Judge Walter Cahoon upheld Judge Small's ruling and included five more petitioners to the original ten. All persons now denied access could be given the right to travel one of two north-south roads when a decision is handed down.

The road travels through the Pine Island Club property which is just north of the Currituck-Dare line which belongs to Earl Slick of Winston Salem, North Carolina. The road sort of parallels what is known as the old pole road and goes on to Poyner's Hill.

Another road constructed by Slick and going through his property also runs through land owned by Coastland Corporation. This road is blocked by a guardhouse and armed guards.

Judge Cahoon's order affects the first road. Hugh Cannon is the lawyer for the petitioners, and he is a partner of Terry Sanford.

Earl Slick was at the hearing with six attorneys. Mr. Carl White told me back when this was going on that Mr. Slick was on a big yacht with friends. He didn't want anybody to see him getting off that big yacht in Coinjock, so he got off in Wilmington and had somebody pick him up there and take him to Currituck.

The state took over the road in 1984 as an extension of NC 12 from Duck to Corolla.

BILL HOLLAN'S ACCOUNT

As I've told you before, Bill Hollan was Mr. Earl Slick's right hand man. The following is his written account of his recollection of what went on about the road:

Sometime in late 1972 or early 1973, Mr. Slick had a meeting at Narrows Island with some of the Currituck County Commissioners, including H.D. Newbern, chairman. According to Mr. Slick, they told him about the Currituck Plan, a joint effort by the state and the county to outline the way in which the Currituck Outer Banks should be developed. The plan called for development to be clustered with sufficient density to allow both the creation of significant areas of open space and the provision of water and sewer-utility service by the developers. It was hoped that there would be significant protected areas.

Prior to the Currituck Plan, Currituck County had a fairly rudimentary subdivision ordinance, consistent with its history as a relatively slow-growing agricultural county. Much of the Currituck Outer Banks had already been platted into relatively small grid lots to be served by individual wells and septic tanks, with little open space. Many of these were "paper" subdivisions without even roads having been constructed or improved. The lots had been sold primarily to buyers from the Virginia Beach area who were accustomed to reaching the lots by driving down the beach from Sandbridge through the Back Bay Wildlife Refuge and the Virginia False Cape State Park. In fact, a toll road commission had been established, and there were plans for a toll road to be built through Back Bay and False Cape.

At the time of Mr. Slick's meeting with the commissioners, access to the Currituck Outer Banks was up in the air. The Department of the Interior had

Picture taken at the bar in Piney Island Club in 2011. *From left to right*: David Swain, original member of Piney Island Club; Bill Hollan, president of Currituck Shooting Club; Travis Morris, original member of Piney Island Club; and Bill Hollan III. *Author's collection.*

announced its intention to restrict or close access through Back Bay. One of the key elements of the Currituck Plan was its recommendation that access be provided across Currituck Sound from mainland Currituck by either ferry service or a bridge to create destination beach development rather than a linear strip. Ben Taylor, one of the consultants involved in the creation of the Currituck Plan, stated that access was the key to the whole plan.

Because of the potential closing of access from the north and the fact that across-sound access would be expensive and was not imminent, the commissioners told Mr. Slick that access across his recently acquired Pine Island property would be the key to their ability to implement the recommendations of the Currituck Plan, which they wanted to do. They hoped to use access to encourage owners of the existing developments to revise their plans for unplatted future portions of their projects and, to the extent possible, to replat existing subdivision areas where significant sales had not already occurred. The two major existing developers were Coastland Corporation (Ocean Sands, James Johnson) and Kabler & Riggs (Carova Beach, North Swan Beach, Swan Beach and Whalehead). What the commissioners asked Mr. Slick to do was to enable them to offer both a carrot and a stick to these two developers and any potential future developers on the Currituck Outer Banks.

The carrot would be to offer to provide access across Pine Island on a reasonable basis in exchange for a willingness to redesign and, to the extent possible, replat existing subdivisions in accordance with the recommendation of the Currituck Plan. The stick would be for Mr. Slick to agree to withhold access from any developer who was unwilling to cooperate with the county's efforts to implement the Currituck Plan. This access was to be temporary until access by ferry or bridge would be provided at some future time.

Mr. Slick told them that he really didn't want any more access through Pine Island than already existed and that, prior to acquiring Pine Island, he had an extensive title search done to determine whether anyone had a right to access through Pine Island. He had gotten a title opinion backed up by title insurance indicating that he had the right to control or prohibit any such access. After further discussion, he said he would attempt to support the county in its effort to implement the Currituck Plan and provide the stick and carrot incentives they had requested.

Soon thereafter, Mr. Slick met with James Johnson and Sam Riggs to discuss terms upon which he would be willing to provide them access to their developments across Pine Island. First, they would have to be willing to comply with the county's desire that they redesign, replat and provide water and sewer service. Second, they would have to construct an access road across Pine Island at their expense and to maintain, patrol and, if necessary, fence the road at their expense. For the easement, Johnson would pay $100,000 and Kabler & Riggs, given their significantly larger properties, would pay $120,000. If other public access were ever provided, Mr. Slick would have the right to terminate the easements by refunding the payments. Johnson agreed to the proposed terms. Sam Riggs uttered an expletive and walked out of the meeting.

During 1973, Mr. Slick entered into an agreement with Johnson along the terms outlined above. The agreement provided that long-term residents of Corolla and their guests and invitees (those who had traditionally been permitted to cross Pine Island) were to be given free use of the road and Mr. Slick would have the right to grant additional easements to other developers (Kabler & Riggs, etc.), subject to their agreeing to share in the cost of constructing, maintaining and patrolling the road.

The right of way for the new road was laid out by Carl White. The meandering course was determined by the location of various areas where ducks concentrated on the property and was designed to prevent disruption of the areas to the maximum extent possible. Coastland (Johnson) redesigned its property in accordance with the Currituck Plan, with provisions for water, sewer and open space.

During 1974, Kabler & Riggs determined that they would need to make arrangements to get an easement from Mr. Slick and obtain the right to use the new so-called Coastland Road across Pine Island. They agreed to comply with the county's revised development ordinances. Their previous intransigence proved costly, as Mr. Slick raised the price for the easement from $120,000 to $500,000, with $120,000 to be paid immediately and the balance to be paid over time with interest. The easement provided that it could be terminated when other public access by road or ferry (120 cars per day minimum) was provided. In that event, the proceeds would not be refunded to Kabler & Riggs.

Subsequently, Mr. Slick offered to contribute $1 million to the state toward the cost of a ferry or bridge, but the offer was never accepted.

Kabler & Riggs also had to deal with James Johnson in connection with the use of the Slick Easement/Coastland Road.

Kabler & Riggs never replatted any of their properties and never installed any water or sewer facilities, seeking instead to persuade the county to abandon the Currituck Plan and revert to individual lots with well and septic tanks. Because of this, Johnson contended that he had been put at a severe competitive disadvantage. As a result, there was continual controversy over access and the use of the road, which was controlled by Johnson.

Unplatted portions of the Kabler & Riggs properties were subsequently sold to other developers who did install water and sewer and did set aside open spaces as called for in the Currituck Plan.

Meanwhile, there were others who contended that Mr. Slick had no right to control access across Pine Island property, arguing that there was already a public road or a neighborhood public road across the property that had been used by the public for years prior to Mr. Slick's acquisition of Pine Island. The question came to a head in the case of Margaret M. West et al. versus Earl F. Slick et al., which was filed in 1975 or 1976. Given the sentiment in Currituck County, the case was moved to Pasquotank County, where the trial occurred in September 1976. After several days of testimony by witnesses for the petitioners, the case was dismissed on September 30, 1976, by Judge Sam Ervin Jr. on the grounds that the evidence, even if considered in the light most favorable to the petitioners, was not sufficient to justify a jury verdict in their favor. The verdict was appealed and upheld by the Court of Appeals on January 18, 1983. The case was further appealed to the State Supreme Court, which, on February 27, 1985, reversed the decision of the Appeals Court, finding that the judge should have allowed the case to continue; however, by that time, the issue was moot because the state had condemned the road in October or November 1984.

John W. Austin

I first met Mr. Johnny Austin when Mr. Adams gave the Boy Scouts a week in the Currituck Beach Coast Guard station in 1947.

In the afternoon, when it was time for the mail boat, we all went over to Mr. Johnny's store to get a bar of candy and a drink and also to see if we had any mail. That's also when I met his son Norris, who was several years younger than me. I'm glad to say we've been friends ever since.

I've told you already about me getting Norris to get his real estate salesman's license and me putting my broker license in Mr. Johnny's store.

As I've said earlier, I took people across the sound in my gas boat *Rhonda* from Waterlily to Corolla when I was developing Corolla Village. Mr. Johnny had an old outhouse out by the store. I don't care how sophisticated some of those people might have been, both men and women, they were glad to see Mr. Johnny's outhouse. Restroom facilities have always been a problem in Corolla.

The information on Mr. Johnny comes from personal knowledge, Mama's scrapbooks and some things I remember from Daddy's files.

One day in the 1970s, I took my tape recorder over to Corolla with me. Shirley Austin must have been with me, too, because sometimes I hear her ask Mr. Johnny a question. We were out under the trees and you can hear the birds chirping.

Mr. Johnny said he and his wife were the only people who had lived through Corolla's heyday. They watched Mr. Knight have his mansion built, which had the first swimming pool and French bidet on the Outer Banks.

John W. Austin. *Author's collection.*

Mr. Johnny said, "They were society people. They had more money than they had time. They got fed up in the North. They built the place to get away from people, but they had good hearts in 'em, especially the old man." Mr. Johnny said Mrs. Knight was a bit eccentric.

He was a notary public and he remembered one time, he was called up to the mansion to notarize a paper. He said she balked: "I'll kiss the cross or count my beads, but I don't swear for no damn man."

He told me that when he was still a boy, he ran a battery rig for Guggenheim, who had a place up around Penny Hill. Before my office burned, I remember seeing one of Daddy's files on Guggenheim. Daddy represented him for something.

Mr. Johnny said he spent a year in France and England during World War I: "When I got back home things were pretty dull, so I went to Washington, D.C., and got me a job. I weren't satisfied and decided I never would be, so I quit and came on home. Been here ever since."

When he got home, he got the job as Corolla Postmaster. He kept that job for thirty-five years. When he retired, his son Norris got the job.

Mary Regan wrote in the Sunday October 25, 1970 *News & Observer*: "Today Corolla has a tiny post office with a grocery store hooked on. On its ten shelves are cans of evaporated milk, sardines, green beans, apple sauce, and grape jam."

MAN OF THE BANKS

1953

(From Mama's Scrapbook; no source reference)

John Austin is a man of the banks. Except for serving during World War I, and a brief residence in Washington, D.C., he has never lived away from

John Austin driving school bus in 1956. *Courtesy Mama's scrapbook.*

the sand and sound of the North Carolina surf. He is postmaster at Corolla and operates the store in which the post office is located. He also drives the Corolla school bus. He was born in Hatteras when his father was assistant keeper of the lighthouse at that point. In 1891 when he was 13 months old, John came to live in the quarters of the Currituck Lighthouse to which his father had been transferred as keeper. For 30 years John lived at the lighthouse, and as a boy he mowed his family's portion of the surrounding lawn, all of which has been long grown over with weeds and shrubs.

In 1935 Austin became Corolla's postmaster. Six days a week the mail comes across Currituck Sound from Churches Island on the mainland. Served by this post office are approximately 22 families from the Virginia State line to Corolla.

To carry out his duties as driver of the school bus, Austin drives along the beach as far north as Penny Hill, about six miles above Corolla. There he picks up pupils, and a few south of that settlement, until there are ten students in his Jeep station wagon. Only severe storms and hurricanes, which make the beach impassable, cancel his trips. Considering the difficulty encountered to attend school in this manner, the students lose very little time.

ANOTHER ARTICLE ON MR. JOHNNY

Gwen White (March 19, 1975)

(From Mama's Scrapbook; no other source reference)

COROLLA—*Johnny Austin, who has been traveling the beach of the Currituck Outer Banks since 1891, said he did not think he would ever see beach access to Virginia closed to vehicular traffic.*

The Corolla native says he "fought the Kaiser for freedom in the first World War" and now he does not have the freedom to travel. "I've seen so much crookedness in my life, it's disgusting to see it now."

Austin, who will be 84 in July, operates the only store on the Currituck Beach. He averages about one trip weekly for stock for his store.

Although he is one of the dozen beach residents who can still cross the Back Bay National Wildlife Refuge, that access is severely limited. Department of Interior Officials have closed the refuge from 9:00 pm to 6:00 am daily and only family vehicles of those who have permits may use the beach across the 4.2-mile refuge.

Refuge officials closed the refuge on the claim vehicles damage the beach, causing erosion and destroying nesting areas of various waterfowl and marine life.

Austin believes the solution is simple. "If they want people off the beach, they could go ahead and hard-surface the three miles." Already a stretch of a little over a mile is surfaced.

"There is no wildlife there since they took over, except a little muskrat," he says.

"They blame cars for destroying the beach, but they're doing more trouble." Austin says. "They put sand fences at the water and the ocean takes the beach away. We always had a flat beach. We never lost more than 100 feet since I've been here and yet they spend millions and lose beach at Virginia. It's cutting away all the time."

Austin believes sand fences should not be built closer than 2,000 yards from the ocean. "Nature looks after itself," he said.

Austin remembers when hunting ducks and geese for sale was a major livelihood of residents on the Currituck Sound. "Then we were allowed eight ducks and four geese per season. [It should have read per day] *Now we can kill three ducks and one goose." He cites dying grass in the marshes as one reason the goose population is declining.*

Sand fences on the beach in 1952. *Courtesy Mama's scrapbook.*

Milfoil on the sound waters is another, he believes, which is why waterfowl are going to the fields for food. "I wouldn't be surprised if in five years we will have a famine caused by birds eating the crops as the locusts did."

Action by the refuge officials to close the refuge has cut off Austin's business. "I'm going to have to close my business," he said. "They can't come in, but I would stay open if things were different." Most of his customers were non-resident property owners or an occasional tourist who stopped at Corolla.

The alternative route to non-resident property owners who wish to reach their property is a trip from Virginia down N.C. 168 and US 158 through Currituck County to Kitty Hawk and then north again by way of Duck and the beach. Access in this direction is by way of Ocean Sands development which permits property owners to pass through to their lots to the north.

As long as Mr. Johnny lived he was kinda the mayor of Corolla. I always enjoyed sitting out under the live oaks talking to him.

I remember one time, I was going to rig me up a little set net to fish in the ocean, just to catch enough fish to eat. He told me to make the net thirty yards long. He said, "That's as far as you can wade out." That's how long I made it, and of course, he was right. I put an anchor on the beach, waded the net out as far as I could on low tide and anchored that end. I had a long line tied around the fluke end of the anchor so I could pull the anchor up. I carried this line back to the shore up current of the net and anchored it on the shore with plenty of slack in it. At high tide, I'd hook my Jeep to that line and pull the net in. This works the same way with the commercial fishermen. They just have a longer net and a dory to take it out to sea.

Now you know how to set a net in the ocean.

Corolla Lighthouse: A Real Blessing

July 15, 1973

(From Mama's Scrapbook; no other source references)

The huge three-masted schooner plunges deep in a trough, her bow awash. Slowly, too slowly perhaps, she breaks free from the angry Atlantic's grasp and prepares to meet another. The ship's master, sailing unfamiliar waters, squints anxiously through sheets of wind-whipped rain. His sextant, rendered useless by the boiling gray storm clouds, hangs idle below deck. Treacherous Outer Banks shoals are very much on the captain's mind as he braces himself for another towering wave. Suddenly, a cry is heard from the forward crow's nest: "Corolla Light on starboard bow!!!" Far in the distance a valiant beacon cuts through the storm. Shouted orders to the helmsman bring the endangered ship back on course. Her captain cast a respectful glance at the lighthouse, silently thankful for its presence.

Construction on the Corolla lighthouse began 100 years ago. High thick grass in Currituck Sound forced builders to use an old Mississippi Riverboat, the "Brooklyn" for transporting materials from Norfolk. [The Brooklyn is sunk west of between northwest and southeast Jones Islands. Wilson Snowden had somebody from East Carolina University up here that wanted to dive on it. Hambone and I took them in my gas boat Rhonda and Hambone told me where to stop. The divers went overboard and found it not ten feet from the gas boat.]

Pilings 40 feet long were sunk in a 100 foot circle for the lighthouse base. A four inch layer of concrete was then poured for its foundation.

Corolla Lighthouse.
Courtesy Mama's scrapbook.

In 1875 the 163 foot high brick tower was completed. Two keepers' houses were also built on the 31 acre tract.

Six wicks, filled with kerosene, were used to generate 65,000 candlepower in those days. A ten gallon tank lasted one night, and light keepers were required to be certain the container was topped off before going to bed. When the sun rose fluted ground glass lenses, made in Germany at a cost of $35,000, filtered the intense light.

A clockwork mechanism, similar to that which powers pendulum clocks, slowly revolved the huge lens. Keepers were kept busy cleaning kerosene smoke from the glass and making certain that the wicks were neatly trimmed.

During the day, men in the "Lighthouse service" polished the light's brass fittings and carefully washed its lens. Two shifts, one beginning at sunset, the other at midnight, assured that one keeper would always be watching the mechanism as it swung across the Atlantic.

In 1933 generators were installed at the light. Workmen dutifully removed the polished brass reflectors and left behind four, 259 watt lamps. Three years later the keepers were also reassigned and Corolla's light was officially designated an "unmanned" post by the Coast Guard.

Left: Hambone showing the diver where the old *Brooklyn* is sunk. Picture is taken in 2000. *Author's collection.*

Below: Diving on the old Mississippi River boat *Brooklyn* that brought the bricks from Norfolk to build the Currituck Beach Lighthouse. I took this picture in 2000. *Author's collection.*

When commercial power lines were strung across the shifting dunes to Corolla in 1956, the lighthouse was wired in. A giant 1,000 watt bulb producing 50,000 candlepower was installed.

Today the quaint keeper's quarters have been stripped of everything that can be carried away. One of the houses has collapsed and is partially overgrown with trees and vegetation.

The Department of the Interior gave 30 of the light's original 31 acres to the North Carolina Conservation Department in 1938. Now the lighthouse stands on a little less than one acre.

Without the constant attention of full-time keepers, the main tower has begun to show its age. Mortar joints are drying, leaving only brown-gray dust behind.

The ornate iron railings that spiral to the light itself have become caked with a hundred years of paint. Most of the original brass clockwork equipment was removed long ago and only an empty glass casing remains.

The original lens is still in place; however, it no longer revolves. A three second flash of light followed by 17 seconds of darkness now replaces the old swinging beam pattern so familiar to seaman of another era.

Lightning struck the tower in 1904, and its scars are still visible on a shattered steel window frame.

Shipping lanes now lie nearly 20 miles from the Corolla light and is barely visible to crews on huge freighters. Still on dark and blustery nights commercial fishermen operating closer to shore look out for the old light's flash and remember days when its beacon led them home.

Old Residence Gets a New Life

August 1, 1982

VIRGINIAN PILOT ARTICLE

Mason Peters

(From Mama's Scrapbook)

The young mayor of Manteo, a Rockefeller heiress and three other friends have signed a lease that will allow them to live together for 50 years in an archly Victorian lighthouse keeper's residence on the wilder shores of Currituck's Outer Banks.

But before any eyebrows are elevated, it should be known the five householders are involved in behavior so impeccable, and in a cause so worthy, that they probably will be honored by the federal government and cheered by preservationists before their half-century leasehold has run out.

The five friends are restoring the neglected gingerbread house that generations of Corolla lighthouse keepers lived in after the sturdy wooden structure was built of heart-pine and cyprus in 1876.

There is a curious thread of inevitability in the restoration that links past and present in the person of John Wilson, the 29 year old mayor of Manteo.

"When we looked at that old building back in 1978, we knew what had to be done," Wilson said last week.

Manteo's cultured mayor has deep roots in the Outer Banks. His great-grandfather, Homer Treadwell Austin, lived in that lighthouse keeper's residence at Corolla almost a century ago. From early days of the country, Austins have been Coast Guardsmen and lighthouse tenders along Carolina's desolate coast.

Right: Mayor John Wilson.
Courtesy Mama's scrapbook.

Below: Old abandoned Currituck
Beach Lighthouse keeper's house.
Courtesy Mama's scrapbook.

Captain Homer Treadwell Austin was assigned twice to keep the Corolla flame. The keeper climbed up 158 feet of literally breathtaking spiral steps to trim the wicks in the enormous lighthouse lantern. Whale oil, and later kerosene, fed the bright fire that could be seen 18 miles at sea.

Wilson's mother had been born by the time Captain Austin served his second duty at the lighthouse, and she remembers playing in a child's wilderness surrounding the lighthouse keeper's home.

But wonders of technology caught up with lighthouse keepers, and since World War II, the bright eye that blinked every 20 seconds atop the tall red tower has sent out the nightly warning without help from human hands. Photocells and failsafe automation have taken the place of wick-trimming.

And the government decided to abandon the lighthouse keeper's residence, which is in reality two identical houses connected so that two keepers and their families could have equal quarters.

In the mid 1950's the General Service Administration gave the duplex structure to North Carolina. Only a tiny plot where the lighthouse stands remains federal property.

When Congress conveyed the property to the state, it was stipulated that the entire 395 foot strip of land running from Currituck Sound to the sea should be used for "recreation and other public purposes."

At the time the state acquired the land, the old keeper's house had by some loving effort ended up on the National Register of Historic Places, which meant North Carolina was charged with preserving the structure.

"When we first looked it over," Mayor Wilson said, "the building had been pretty well stripped. The mantels were gone, and some of the stairways and banisters. All the windows had been carried away. But even with years of exposure to the weather, the building was sound. It was cypress and heart pine."

And that sturdy wood still carries faint writing in flowing Victorian script on every major timber, sill, rafter and joist. The double house (and another one just like it that still stands in Charleston, S.C.) had been prefabricated by the Coast Guard on some distant mainland, disassembled and later reconstructed "by the numbers" on an immensely strong basement foundation in Corolla.

"Vines had come in through empty windows, and one of them trailed up the stairs and finally found a way out through the roof," Wilson recalled.

Wilson joined with the four friends to find a way to restore what to him was a family homestead.

Outer Banks Conservation was incorporated as a non-profit organization to deal with the state in plans to renovate the house.

Officers of the corporation in addition to Wilson, are William M. Parker, a Raleigh landscape architect; Ann G. Bahr, who works with the architect of the Capital in Washington; Meile Rockefeller, granddaughter of Nelson Rockefeller and daughter of Rodman Rockefeller of New York; and Lee Salet, whose roots are in the Outer Banks, but who now lives in California. "All of us are either 28 or 29," Wilson said.

Not long ago, Anne Bahr married Philipe Jacquet, a French lawyer, at the house the friends are restoring. "It was beautiful; just beautiful," said Wilson of the wedding scene.

The Mayor at various times had met the four friends when he was studying at Harvard, George Washington University and the University of North Carolina, at Chapel Hill.

After a complicated journey through tangles of bureaucracy, Wilson and the corporation reached an agreement with North Carolina Resources Commission, holder of title to the property.

The state agreed to anti up $25,000 in restoration money provided the corporation would match the funds equally. The corporation did.

But $50,000 was not nearly enough to re-build the century old structure, so the state worked out an unusual "lease" whereby the five preservationist will finish the job with their own money in exchange for "residential privileges" in the house for 50 years.

"The house belongs to the state," said Wilson, "and when we finish, we want people to be able to see it. It will be regularly open like a special kind of museum."

For now, the friends discourage visitors, except on the ground floor, and even there with much cautioning. As in any old and torn up building, there are pitfalls and traps dangerous to the unwary.

Wilson, who is largely responsible for much of the Elizabethan restoration of downtown Manteo, works at the old building "every weekend opportunity that I have." Sometimes it is a thankless chore, he says. For instance, it is agonizing to him not to know what the original stairwells and banisters looked like.

"Somebody took them, and so far we haven't been able to find the plans for the building in the National Archives in Washington," he explained. Wilson and his associates would be delighted to hear from any history buff who might know where the old house was fabricated before being knocked down for the trip to Corolla.

The partners have cleaned up and landscaped the overgrown yard around the house, uncovering in the process the double brick walkways that are a feature of the dual accommodations

Wilson says he does not have the faintest idea how long it will take the friends to finish restoring the house.

It does me good to see this house and the Whalehead Club in the condition they are in today. In the early 1970s, I never thought to see them look like they do today.

Norris Austin

Norris has now taken his place as the old man in Corolla. His mother and daddy have long been dead. His older brother, Otley, retired from the Coast Guard and moved back to Corolla. He and his wife, Maizie, are both dead now. Norris never married.

Norris owns the Austin building in Corolla where Winks', Corolla Post Office, Riggs Realty and one or two take-out restaurants are located. Norris lives over top of the post office. His health is not good, and he had an elevator installed last year to get him up to his house.

I'm not going to interview Norris. I don't need to interview him. I'm five years older than he is. I've known and been friends with him since he was about seven years old. He has been interviewed to death. He has been written about in newspapers and books, and *Our State* magazine (it used to be called the *State* magazine) even had a spread on him.

The next thing is he can't hear it thunder, and I'm nearly as bad. My wife has a house on Persimmon Street in Corolla Village she rents out in the summer. In the winter, we spend right many weekends there and go to church at Corolla Chapel. Norris sits on the back row in the wing where he has a special hearing device. Jo Ann and I sit right ahead of him. We don't talk a lot in church before the service starts because we have to holler at each other, and that don't go over good in church.

Norris has a long-distance relationship with a woman in Jacksonville, Florida. I only know her as Bunnie. She has children there and won't move up here, and he is not going to leave Corolla to live in Florida. They talk on

Above: Three old friends at Heritage Day in
October 2008 at the Whalehead Club. Travis
Morris, Dot Jones (whose family owns Jones' dock
in Waterlily) and Norris Austin. *Author's collection.*

Right: Norris Austin at Corolla Post Office in
1970. *Courtesy Mama's scrapbook.*

the phone at least once a day. She comes
up here some, and I don't know if he
goes down there now or not. I may write
him and ask him. I can't holler at him in
church on Sunday about that.

What I am going to do for you about
Norris is give you an article by Mary
Regan in the Sunday, October 25, 1970
News & Observer from Mama's scrapbook:

THE POSTMASTER

"What we need worse than anything else is a school." The speaker is 30-year-old Norris, Mr. Austin's blue-eyed bachelor son. "There's one family of little girls up there. Every time I see them, they ask, 'Are we going to start school next year?' It's pitiful."

The state pays $25 per month per child in lieu of transportation. Corolla residents laugh at the $25. They say that unless a family has relatives near a school it would be impossible to bed and board a child on that amount.

On the wall of the store hangs a petition. Sixteen families representing 31 children have signed. It reads: "If schooling were available, I would be interested in living in the Outer Banks Area."

Like his father, Norris, too, left Corolla once. He joined the Coast Guard but was processed out after six weeks when his arches fell. "I had never walked on pavement before," he teased.

He attended business school in Virginia and worked six months with the FBI. "But I wanted to feel the sand between my toes," he said. So he came home and became postmaster when his father retired.

His mind is zeroed in on the future. Development plans are tacked to the wall of the store and he thinks Corolla's road has been too long in coming. Norris likes peace and privacy that a roadless location brings. But, Corolla is invaded by so many beach buggies as it is that he feels residents might as well profit by the invasion.

All Corolla residents do not agree. They're divided almost down the middle about the road. Norris's cousin, Gene Austin, is on the other side. He is the tall dark caretaker of the mansion. Some Corolla residents say that his joke-loving wife, Shirley, is its ghost.

They're fortyish. Their three daughters, ages 16, 12, 10, have bunked in with Shirley's relatives across the sound for all their schooling. They come home on weekends.

Since the trip to school overland is 50 miles, Gene usually takes the girls five miles across the sound in his 26 foot cabin boat. The trip takes 16 minutes.

It's a good thing it doesn't last longer. Gene was discharged from the Coast Guard because of chronic sea sickness. He returned to Corolla when the mansion's caretaker retired.

He sees advantages and disadvantages to a paved road, but "in a way, I hate to see it come in," he said. "It'll ruin the place. We've got one of the best beaches on the East Coast. But, the road will come. It's really going

My gas boat *Rhonda* at Jones' dock in Waterlily. *Author's collection.*

to force itself in. It's just a matter of time, because you can't stop progress. Still I hate to see it.

Gene and Shirley Austin

I'm going to insert one little story about Gene and Shirley here while I'm thinking about it.

When Atlantic Research was still at Whalehead testing rocket fuel, I was hunting with my float box in Lighthouse Bay. At the time, I had a 442 Oldsmobile in my gas boat *Rhonda*. It had two bolts that held the shaft in the coupling. One of those bolts broke. I eased over to the end of the airstrip. They had "No Trespassing" signs all over the place. I knew Gene and Shirley were working there. Shirley saw me and drove down to the end of the airstrip to pick me up. She took me up to the shop and we found a bolt that would work.

When Atlantic Research was gone and I was developing over there, I had built a little dock near the end of the airstrip so when the tide was real low, I could tie up there.

Gene had been to the hospital with kidney colic but was back home, and I got a call from Shirley. She wanted me to come across the sound and pick them up. Gene was in terrible pain. I think he couldn't urinate. The wind was blowing a living gale from the northeast. I told her I'd come right on. She said she'd call the rescue squad to meet us at Jones' Dock in Waterlily.

I went straight to Waterlily, jumped in *Rhonda* and hurried on across the sound. When I got to the outside dock, Gene, Shirley and the girls were all waiting for me in their Jeep.

I got them all loaded up, with Gene and the girls in the forward cabin. He was doubled up in pain. Shirley and I were standing under the shelter cabin where I was running the boat. As I said, it was blowing a gale and really rough. About the time we got to the Gull Rock, which is about in the middle of the sound, we heard a "pow." I looked at Shirley and she looked at me, but we neither said anything. I still had that Oldsmobile engine in *Rhonda*, and we both knew one of those bolts had popped. By now I had sense enough to take spare bolts but didn't want to stop out there and have to put them in. I never slacked up on her and the other bolt held until we made it to the dock. The Man Upstairs was looking after us. The rescue squad was waiting. End of story.

Deputy Sheriff Griggs O'Neal

When I first knew Griggs, he lived in one of the houses Mr. Adams had moved up to the Whalehead Club compound from Poyner's Hill after World War II. Griggs and his wife, Louise, lived in the house near the gate to the road that goes by the lighthouse. Shirley and Gene Austin lived in the identical house by the arched bridge.

I first got to know Griggs when I started developing Corolla Village for Kenyon Wilson, Carl White and Stewart Hume. Griggs had a six-wheel drive army truck. Hambone and I hauled the material for the first two oceanfront houses built in Corolla across Currituck Sound from Waterlily to the boat basin at the Whalehead Club. We loaded it on Griggs's army truck, and he carried it out to the beach.

We needed ditches dug for drainage in Corolla Village. We got Calvin Bright, from Elizabeth City to bring his dragline to Corolla to do the work. The problem was getting the dragline to Corolla. Calvin had a Chevrolet truck and lowboy trailer he hauled his dragline on. We got Griggs to meet him at the beginning of the pole road with his army truck to pull him, and Calvin had somebody with a bulldozer to push him.

Above: Griggs O'Neal's army truck pulling Calvin Bright's Chevrolet truck and lowboy trailer with his dragline. The bulldozer is pushing. *Author's collection.*

Left: Taking dragline up the pole road. *Author's collection.*

NEWS & OBSERVER

Sunday, October 25, 1970

(From Mama's Scrapbook)

Griggs O'Neal is Corolla's guitar-playing deputy sheriff. He's bashful about performing. He only plays "when I get the urge. Sometimes on patrol on the beach I just pull over and play."

One day a paved highway will come to Corolla. And this six-dog five family town will be history.

Griggs O'Neal playing guitar. His wife, Louise, is in the background. *Courtesy Mama's scrapbook.*

His humor is deadpan. A sign in his yard says "Unmarked police cars patrolling." He gestured, straight-faced and stern, at his truck out front. Then the dead-pan broke. "Somebody throwed it out on the beach," he explained. He has the nonchalant bravery of small-framed men who don't waste much time thinking about how small they are. "I was called out one morning", he began, "It was just as foggy as it could be. There were 19 boys on the beach, five carloads. They'd run through a fence my neighbor had and they were after a hog with a sledge hammer. Drinking, hollering and carrying on right close to the house."

"He forgot his gun," his wife volunteered.

"Yeah," he agreed. "I forgot and left my gun at the house." They had the license plates all sanded up. I sent up and brushed them off and started writing them down.

They didn't try to harm me a bit. I just told them they could move on or there'd be somebody else there to help me. Now, some of them same boys come down here. We're good friends. When they get here they come to see me first."

"He was sheriff for a long time and never received a penny," his wife said, with obvious pride.

"I taken it for the sake of having an officer over here," Mr. O'Neal explained. For six years he had a badge, but not a uniform. He got two dollars to serve a warrant; one dollar for a subpoena. He fished on the side. He is now a full fledged deputy, the only law enforcement officer in a 26 mile strip from the Dare County line to Virginia. The jail is 80 miles away.

In the early days the O'Neal's were living with his parents six miles up the beach. In 1962 the freakish Ash Wednesday storm struck.

I'm going to take a little detour here. On the day of the Ash Wednesday storm I was lying in the sleeper of my B-61 Mack truck in Daytona Beach Florida listening to the radio waiting to get a load of baskets unloaded I had brought from Murfreesboro, North Carolina. It came on the radio about how high the tide was in Daytona and told about what was going on in North Carolina.

Of course, there were no cellphones. You young folks reading this won't understand that. I tried to call home and couldn't get through. The lines were down. I was very worried now.

After I got unloaded I went on to Winter Garden Florida and loaded fruit for New York City. There was no Chesapeake Bay Bridge Tunnel then. We rode the ferry. The tollbooth to get on the ferry was at least five hundred feet from the ferry dock. I saw on a television that water was up to the running board on a truck at the tollbooth. That really had me worried because I had no communication with my family, and I was worried about their well being. As I got closer to home the phone and light lines were down. Thankfully, when I got home, my family was OK.

My in-laws Walton and Birdye Meiggs had an oceanfront cottage in Kill Devil Hills. My first wife, Frances (if I haven't told you, she and I were married thirty-eight years and had four children. She died with cancer in 1992. I married Jo Ann Hayman in 1995), and her daddy got as far as a hill in Kitty Hawk on the bypass. The ocean was washing across the bypass beyond this point. The cottage is on stilts, and the ocean can go and come. The only damage was that it washed the gas bottles out from under the house and messed up the cement in the driveway.

Now back to Griggs O'Neal.

"Louise and my father were in the house," Mr. O'Neal recalls. "I had two ponies, a cow and a calf in a stable. I went out there with my mother to

turn them out to the pasture. Then the tide came in. It was over your head in places. Mrs. O'Neal joined in. We didn't know if they had drowned or not. We went upstairs and stayed dry. The house washed off its foundation. We just sat there and watched a house come floating by. There were six people in it. All I could think about was that the end had come.

It did come for my mother, Mr. O'Neal said. *We were half-way back to the house when she passed out in my arms. We'd been out there in the pasture for seven hours in water up to here."* He indicates his chest.

"The water temperature was 38 degrees. Some of the hogs that got loose when the fences got washed out stayed free and multiplied. Their offspring are the wild hogs that come out of the myrtle bushes at night and root holes in front yards.

Hog-size boxes, built like a rabbit trap, sit just off the little dirt roads in Corolla. Everybody has his own box. When winter comes and the bacon runs out, somebody goes and sets his trap."

The thousands of hippies who came to watch the eclipse made good conversation for a while, one resident said of their impact on the community.

Mr. O'Neal said, "They didn't cause any serious trouble. They were sort of peaceful." There was a touch of local pride in his voice when he told why they kept coming back. "They're crazy about it," he said. "The water is shallow. They can get out on the beach and camp. Nobody bothers them as long as they behave themselves, as long as they abide by the law."

Wouldn't a paved road bring in problems that Corolla has so far escaped? "It probably will," Mr. O'Neal answered. "But it's going to happen sooner or later. You'd be able to control traffic and stuff better with a road. It'd make it better for people and I'm for anything the majority of people want."

"It'd be nice if we had a little store," Mrs. O'Neal said, a five and ten, something to go to.

"The way the world is building up," Mr. O'Neal went on, "everything's getting crowded. Something has got to open up. People got to build somewhere."

"I'd like to see more people around me," Mrs. O'Neal added.

Griggs and Louise ended up over here in Coinjock on the mainland. I used to see them at the post. They both died over here.

The Pontons

The Pontons didn't want development. They're fishermen. They lived in Norfolk until 1967. They moved to Corolla where it was desolate. They could fish on the beach and not be bothered by tourists.

I met Buddy Ponton in 1970, when I'd see him on the beach. We've been friends ever since. Buddy had a dory with an open shark's mouth with the teeth showing painted on the bow. I've seen Buddy go to sea in that dory when he had no business being in that ocean, but The Man Upstairs was with him because he always made it back to shore.

Buddy and his first wife, Ellen, had two children, Robert and William, I don't remember which is the eldest. Buddy and Ellen divorced. Buddy remarried. His second wife is named Annie. They have a grown son, Edward. He graduated from college and goes on foreign mission trips. He is a really nice young man, and when he is home, he works on the beach. I saw Edward in church on a recent Sunday, and he told me he collects trash and pulls people out that get stuck in the sand in the four-wheel drive area for Twiddy Company Realtors. They have a big rental business up there. Edward told me that William is a chemical engineer in New Bern, North Carolina, and Robert works with some big company in South Carolina. If the preacher at Corolla Chapel is gone, Edward fills in for him.

Buddy finally had to give up fishing in the ocean. The tourists got too thick. It may be just as well; he is getting too old to be doing that anyway. He turned seventy this year (2013). He told me the other day that now

Ponton Fish Company going to sea to set fish net in 1979. *Courtesy Annie Ponton.*

Ponton Fish Company going to sea to set fish net in 1979. *Courtesy Annie Ponton.*

he has a restaurant clientele he furnishes crabs and fish to. He fishes and crabs in Currituck Sound. Annie works for Twiddy & Company, Real Estate.

Now I'm going to share with you a story of the Pontons that was written by Mary Regan, staffwriter for the *News & Observer*, and was in the Sunday, October 25, 1970 paper, from Mama's scrapbook.

> *Up until three years ago, the Pontons lived in Norfolk. There're two families: Mr. and Mrs. Thomas Ponton and their son Andy, 21; and another son, Buddy, 27, and his wife, Ellen.*

The Pontons. *Left to right:* Buddy; his father, Thomas; and his brother, Andy. *Courtesy Annie Ponton.*

"I'll fight the tough going," Mr. Ponton said. *"After 30 years catering to the public, you get tired of it."* Mr. Ponton was a contractor until he retired five years ago. He and his boys started filling in the marsh on the sound side of the banks. They've now built two houses there.

Of her blond boys, Mrs. Ponton said, *"They were born too late. They should have been born in a time when it was really rough."*

Tough going to Mrs. Ponton is really not tough. She's had to learn to use less frozen food and more canned stuff. She had never belonged to clubs, but she does miss her church. She knits and sews and cooks and keeps house. Television reception is better than in Norfolk, she says.

"You have to be able to make your own pleasure."

The only real bother is just having the idea that *"you can't go if you want to,"* she said.

And water. A recent visitor from down the banks drank a glass of water and said, *"I know this is rainwater, because it tastes like shingles."* Other people in Corolla have good water, but the Pontons' is salty and full of sulfur. It turns the bath room and kitchen fixtures black. The only thing they use it for is the toilet.

They do all their washing with rain water that they guide from the roof through troughs into big garbage cans lined with plastic bags.

"Some people think we're out of our tree," she said. *"It takes nerve. But people who come down this beach are people who like this kind of living. People who don't have this are the kind that don't understand."*

Mrs. Ponton's daughter-in-law laughed when she was asked what she did in her spare time. *"Sleep,"* she answered, *"when there's time."*

Sometimes she helps haul in the nets (at three a.m.) and drive the fish to market, an hour away. It's dawn when they finally get to bed.

The Ponton men, like all Corolla men, are duck hunters, but the younger Pontons have an agreement. "I clean anything that swims. He cleans anything that flies," Ellen said.

Before they came to Corolla Buddy had worked part-time as a fisherman. Now, he is hoping to make enough money so he can stay here.

His brother Andy is not quite so committed to the life of a fisherman. He's young and has a mustache, and he's going to try it another year before he makes a final decision.

Mr. Ponton, though, is here to stay. He played semi-pro football, stands a half head taller than his boys and looks just about as hardy. He is an ebullient man who knows what he thinks.

"It takes a little nerve," he admits, to make such a major move, to buy some marshland and start out to make it solid ground. "But fishing satisfies the gambling instinct in a person. You never know what you're going to catch. A catch can bring you $1,000 or nothing."

He and his family are definitely opposed to the road. "If it gets built up around here, I'll go find me an island," he said.

Simply living in Corolla is not sufficient. It's the fishing, too, that counts. "Just come down here and live and not do anything is no good either," Mr. Ponton explained. "Like those fellows in Florida. Waiting for the man with the sickle to catch up. He's got to run to catch up with me."

The men had been working on nets all morning. It was not yet lunch but the sun was hot and Mr. Ponton sent to the house for cold beers.

Noticing a slight hesitation, he boomed out happily, "This is God's country. You can do what you want."

Ponton Fish Company pulling in a net full of fish.
Courtesy Annie Ponton.

Kenyon and Gwendolyn Wilson

I've told you about Kenyon Wilson in the development of the beach. Now, I'm going to tell you a little about him living in Corolla.

After the Occidental Petroleum deal fell through, Kenyon didn't even want to go to Corolla until Gerald Friedman picked up the notes and gave them Corolla Village free and clear.

Now, he wanted me to take him and Gwen over to Corolla. We went over there in my gas boat *Rhonda*. By now, I had an old Jeep I kept at Gene and Shirley's house beside the boat basin.

We got in the Jeep and rode out to the beach. The tide was low, and the beach was wide. It looked just like Daytona. They fell in love with it. We did this several times, and they liked it better each time.

Now I need to give you a little background. Kenyon and his first wife had divorced. She got their house in Pine Lakes in Elizabeth City.

Kenyon and Gwen got married and were living in an apartment over his law office on Riverside Avenue in Elizabeth City. He had three grown sons and a daughter who didn't have much to do with him after the divorce from their mother. Gwen had one grown married daughter that did have a lot to do with them on the phone. She was married to a man in the service and didn't live around here.

Now, they decided they wanted to build a house in Corolla and live there, and he would commute by boat to his law office in Elizabeth City. The first thing he had to have was a boat.

I went to City Marina with them on the causeway in Camden to pick out a boat. Erie Haste was the owner then. The boat was gold. I think it was a Carver about twenty feet long. It had a couple of bunks under the forward deck. Where you steer, it was closed in with canvas. It had a seat for the operator and one across from it. There was a seat back of each of these facing aft. Then it had a seat on each side of the engine box in the stern with drink holders for each seat. It had a Mercruiser inboard-outboard with a six cylinder Chevrolet block. The boat would probably run

Kenyon and Gwendolyn Wilson. *Courtesy Gwendolyn Wilson.*

The boat on the right is the *Gwendolyn-Corolla*. Hambone is going out in his skiff from Jones' Dock in Waterlily. *Author's collection.*

about thirty-five miles per hour. He had "Gwendolyn, Corolla" painted on the transom.

We got the boat and got it over to Jones' Dock in Waterlily. Currituck Sound was full of milfoil. We had paths all through the sound, and of course with all that grass, the sound didn't get rough.

So this was the first trip, maiden voyage, for Kenyon, Gwen and me. We went to the Whalehead Club and tied up in the boathouse in the shade. Kenyon and I were drinking gin and tonics and all of us were talking about the house. Gwen is a teetotaler. She was mixing the drinks. Never again. We ended up with Gwen driving the boat back to Waterlily with Kenyon and me sitting in the seats on either side of the engine box in the stern. That's all I'll say about that.

The next thing they had to have was transportation over there. Kenyon had an old Chevrolet Caprice that he got Caleb Poyner to put big tires on to make a beach buggy.

Now that they had a boat and a beach buggy, they had to have a house. Aubrey Aydlett agreed to build it for them. Jimmy Hayman, (J.I. Hayman Building Hardware and Building Supply in Coinjock) took the material to Jones' Dock in Waterlily, and Hambone and I loaded it on a barge and pulled it with *Rhonda* to Corolla. Griggs O'Neal hauled it out to the beach on his six-wheel drive army truck.

Aubrey bought a gas boat that Bill Snowden had so he could commute. He got some boys together and built the house.

Kenyon and Gwen had a big house in Jacksonville, Florida, in a gated community called Deerwood that was on a golf course.

By this time Corolla Village was selling good. He had a new Mark IV he kept at the airport in Jacksonville, Florida, and one he kept at the airport in Norfolk, Virginia.

The house they built in Corolla was an A-frame and would literally fit in the family room of the house in Florida. It didn't take long to get to Jacksonville on a direct flight. Gwen told me that many times she would buy meat in Elizabeth City, put it in a little cooler and cook it for supper in Jacksonville.

After they got the house built, many times when they went to Jacksonville, Frances and I and the kids would go to their house in Corolla. When they were in Corolla, a lot of times Frances and I would go to Jacksonville.

The weekend of February 14 and 15, 1973, we had a blizzard. The fourteenth was my oldest daughter, Ruth's, fifteenth birthday, and the fifteenth was my son Walton's sixteenth birthday. On this Friday afternoon,

The first house in the picture is the Copeland house. It had been framed up and blew down in the February 1993 blizzard. The second house is the Wilson house, which was the first house built on the oceanfront in Corolla. Third is the old Poyner's Hill Coast Guard station. Mr. Adams had it moved to Whalehead property and made a cottage out of it. Fourth is the old Currituck Beach Coast Guard station. *Author's collection.*

Frances and I and the kids loaded up *Rhonda* and went to Corolla. When we pulled up to the boathouse at the Whalehead Club, Griggs O'Neal met us and said it was snowing at Hatteras. I said, "Aw, it ain't gonna snow here." Thankfully, I'd carried my chain saw to cut wood for the fireplace.

The house had big glass windows in the living room, facing the ocean, all the way to the ceiling. The glass had never come, and they had thick Plexiglas in them at the time.

The snow did come, and so did the wind. I think they said it blew eighty miles per hour the next day. I'll never forget the seas looked like mountains out there. The ocean is shallow along there and the seas were breaking a long way out.

The wind was blowing so hard I was afraid it was going to blow the Plexiglas in. I cut some two-by-fours and nailed them across to strengthen the windows.

Aubrey Aydlett had just framed up a house on an oceanfront lot I sold the Copelands several lots north of Kenyon Wilson's. The wind flattened that. We saw an extension ladder go sailing by in the wind.

Going home three days after the blizzard of 1973. *Author's collection.*

Penny Hill or Lewark Hill (same place). *Author's collection.*

Of course, the power went off early in the ordeal. We did have telephone. They had just put a new system in Corolla that had a generator that came on in case of power failure, and it worked. We stayed in touch with the Wilson's in Florida and Mama in Coinjock.

Our only heat was the fireplace. We had to melt snow for drinking water. My youngest daughter, Rhonda, wasn't thinking and washed her hands in the drinking water. Now we had to melt more snow.

Frances had brought right much food from home already cooked so she wouldn't have to cook so much. The Wilson's told us by phone to use all we could out of their freezer because it would probably have to be thrown out, depending on how long the power was off. We used what we could cook over the fireplace.

The temperature was down in the teens. The boat basin was frozen over, but it didn't make any difference because the tide was so low we couldn't get out anyway. If I remember right, when the wind died out, the sound froze over.

I was afraid to drive up the beach because you couldn't tell how deep the snowdrifts were, and if we got stuck, we'd freeze to death. It was three days before I felt like it was safe for us to drive up the beach and come home.

We had some good times over there. Kenyon drank Old Crow. I remember one time, we had been drinking Old Crow and took the Caprice up to Penny Hill. We backed off and got a good start and ran up that hill.

I don't want to forget to mention the fact that Gwen is a really good cook, and I enjoyed a lot of her meals.

I remember one time, Ambrose Twiford (Hambone) and I were supposed to meet Kenyon early one morning to go duck hunting in Lighthouse pond. At that time, I had the old Russell Griggs boat, which was a thirty-two-foot battery boat built in 1927. That morning, for some reason, we were in that instead of *Rhonda*. The compass was off at least ten degrees on it. That morning, it was so foggy you could hardly see the bow of the boat, but you could look up and see the stars as clear as day.

Hambone was watching the stars and feeling the bottom with his shoving pole. He had fished that sound so much he knew that bottom like the palm of his hand. He would tell me which way to steer and took us right in to the dock. I always said Hambone had a doctorate in Currituck Sound. He knew more about Currituck Sound than anybody I've ever known in my life. He helped me many times guide sportsmen with my float box. We've both swum many a goose. We'd take turns sleeping and swimming geese.

I got carried away talking about my old friend Hambone. Anyway, we went hunting and killed some ducks, then went back to the oceanfront house, and Gwen fixed us a big breakfast.

I looked after Kenyon Wilson's boat; he didn't even know how to check the oil. I remember one time, I had taken it to City Marina to have something done to it. I was by myself when I brought it back and put it over at the Wildlife ramp in Coinjock. The trailer had rollers on it, and when I turned it loose, it came off the trailer so fast I couldn't get it. It was drifting out in the creek that goes in the Intracoastal Waterway. I was really in a mess. The boat had now drifted out in the waterway. About that time, I saw the bilge pump come on. Now I was really in trouble, because I realized they had taken the plug out at the marina. I never thought about them doing that.

That's not all. I looked up, and here comes a yacht down the waterway. Thankfully, it was only about a forty-footer. I waved at him, and he saw my situation. He got hold of the boat and pushed it close enough to shore that I could grab it. That saved the day for me. I was really sweating it when I saw that bilge pump come on, because I knew it would soon run the battery down, and then the boat would sink. Again, The Man Upstairs was with me, as he has been so much of my life.

Renting Houses in Corolla

I told you Hambone and I hauled the lumber from Waterlily to Corolla on a barge to build Kenyon Wilson's house, which was the first house built on the oceanfront in Corolla. They didn't rent that. It was their home. The second house we hauled the lumber for was the Copeland house, which was a few lots north of the Wilson house. I did rent that for them.

The third house on the oceanfront was the old Poyner's Hill Coast Guard station that Mr. Adams had moved from Poyner's Hill up to the Whalehead property, but not on the oceanfront. I sold an oceanfront lot south of the Wilson house to Dr. Moore from Lexington, Kentucky.

Kenyon Wilson gave Dr. Moore the old Poyner's Hill station, and he had it moved out on the oceanfront lot. Dr. Moore got Ronnie Ivey, a carpenter who lived at Maple to renovate the house, and he did a fine job of it.

Ronnie lived on Coinjock Bay less than a quarter of a mile north of me. He just had a skiff, but I'd see him go by every morning going to Corolla to work. There was so much grass in the sound that the sound didn't get rough. We had paths through the grass.

By this time, I'm glad to say that Jimmy Hayman had bought an army truck and was delivering material to Corolla. Hambone and I didn't have to haul it across the sound.

For those of you who don't know where Poyner's Hill station was, it was on the oceanfront right in front of Currituck Shooting Club, which was on the sound front before it burned in 2003. This is also where we got off the pole road and drove the beach north. From this point north to Sandbridge,

Virginia, the beach was flat like Daytona and from there south, it was soft and pebbly.

Let me tell you about the day I sold Dr. Moore that lot. He saw the sign in front of my office in Coinjock that said, "Corolla Property" and came in. It was raining, but he wanted to go see it anyway. We went to Waterlily and got in my gas boat *Rhonda* and went to Corolla. I just knew I was wasting my time. It was raining so hard I docked inside the boathouse. I still had that Corvair with "Currituck Realty" written on the side with white shoe polish. We got in that, and I wound her up for us to go out to the oceanfront. She'd go good as long as you stayed up out of the tracks and didn't get it hung up underneath. It was raining so hard we couldn't get out of the Corvair. I just pointed to the lot and showed him on a plat where it was. We went back and got in the boat, and as I said, I just knew I was wasting my time. He told me he'd take the lot. I got a contract out of my briefcase and wrote it up right there on top of the engine box. The contract was just one page. Now a contract for a vacant lot is seven pages just for the contract plus all the other papers you have to have.

Dr. Moore told me he bought in Sanibel Island, Florida, when it was about like Corolla. It had gotten so built up he wanted to move out. He said he figured he'd have ten years in Corolla before it built up. This was in 1971 or '72.

I rented Dr. Moore's house, and I rented the Copeland house. I took the renters across the sound in the boat with all their luggage, groceries, etc. I also picked up their garbage twice a week and brought it back to the mainland. If they wanted or needed anything, they'd call me, no cellphones—there was a payphone at the post office.

I'll never forget the first people I rented Dr. Moore's house to. They stayed two weeks. It was Gordon and Gwen Cruickshanks. They had another couple with them whose names I can't recall, but I do remember he was an FBI agent assigned to Mamie Eisenhower as a bodyguard. His wife was a very attractive Swedish woman.

It took two boats to take all their gear. I had my son Walton helping me. He doesn't say much, but he asked them if they left anything home. The Cruickshanks later moved to Currituck and spent the rest of their lives here.

I had the opportunity to have had a good real estate and rental business in Corolla. When the road came, the real estate agents came like fleas on a dog's back, which I knew they would. If any of our children had been interested in real estate, Frances and I would probably have built an office in Corolla, but since none of them were interested, we decided we could make a living on the mainland and make enough money to live like we wanted to.

Frances and I started Currituck Realty with a trailer as an office in 1970. That's all we could afford at the time, and the reason it sits on an angle is it was in the corner of my daddy's racetrack. My daddy was not a gambler, but he loved horses like I love boats. After he retired as a superior court judge he built a half-mile racetrack here beside the house.

My first trailer burned in the March 1 snowstorm of 1980. By this time, my daddy had died, and I'd plowed the racetrack up. If the children had been interested, we would probably have built an office then. They were not interested, and the quickest thing to do was put another trailer there. It's like me; it's old now, but I hope it will last me out.

I used to have the only real estate office in Currituck. Then, when things started getting better, agents came from Elizabeth City, Virginia, and the beach and built big offices. I used to know about everybody; now I hardly know anybody. My office is not good enough to get agents to work with me now. They want to go with the big companies. Well that's enough of all that.

Faye Barco Hooper

Faye said she remembered going to the Whalehead Club with her Mama when she was a little girl to clean the house. She said the local people were hired to clean the house, and she was given a dollar bill, which was a lot of money in the 1930s.

She remembered going there when Miss Grace and Mr. Cleveland Lewark were caretakers. The names Faye remembers from Corolla were Bowden, White, Beasley, Austin and Mr. Saul Sanderlin, who was the postmaster.

Faye said the school didn't seem so small, but she was small. Miss Coward was the schoolteacher in Corolla. Faye didn't know why, but Miss Coward let Faye go to school before she was old enough. She'd let her go to the blackboard and do problems. The school was one room, but it was full.

Faye said they had a place in the back where they fixed lunch, and one of the things she remembered them fixing was corned beef hash.

She remembered Mr. Parker's store and Mr. Henley's store. She said it was between the school and the beach. It was in the area behind the school, but not directly (probably in the area where Twiddy's office is now). They would play out in the sand dunes, and there were wild grapes growing there.

Faye remembers going to Virginia Beach one time. Her daddy didn't have a car at that time. She said somebody must have taken them. She remembered a blind man on the street with a cup full of pencils. Her dad picked up a pencil and then put it back in the cup. He said something to the man and then put something in his cup. Faye said it's strange how you remember little things like that. Virginia Beach seemed like a mighty big

Grissie Barco and his daughter, Faye. Behind them is the gate to the Knight's Corolla Island, now the Whalehead Club. Faye said they didn't have a camera and this is the only picture she has. *Courtesy Faye Barco Hooper.*

place to her. When she lived in Corolla, she never remembers going south. They always went north to Virginia.

Faye was born on Spry Creek in Corolla in what was her uncle Tillman Lewark's house. She said there was a little bridge across Spry Creek. The midwife who delivered her was Margaret (Lady Bug) Bowden. She remembered a girl about her age going to school named Jeannie Bowden.

Faye said when she lived in Corolla she didn't realize how remote it was and it didn't seem like a small place then. She said they were really in the real outback and didn't realize it.

When her daddy didn't have a car, he had a gas boat (inboard motorboat). She remembers one time, her daddy and mama took her in the gas boat to Poplar Branch to Dr. Griggs to get a smallpox vaccination. She still has the receipt signed by Dr. Griggs.

Faye remembers when her daddy would take her and her mama to Poplar Branch, and somehow they'd catch the bus to Beaufort where her mama was from. She doesn't know how it was connected, but they would come back on the bus, and her daddy would be there in the boat to pick them up.

Later her daddy got a job at Moon's Shipyard, and they moved to Norfolk. She said that was like being in New York City. They lived there awhile and then moved to Back Bay, and she went to school in Creeds, Virginia.

About this time, Grissie Barco, Faye's daddy, worked out some kinda deal with her uncle Tillman Lewark to get the house on Spry Creek.

By this time, her daddy had some kind of old car but didn't have a gas boat. When her daddy was dickering to get her uncle Till's house, they drove down there one day and spent the night. It was late when they were going home the next day, and they had to have the lights on. Everybody around here had to have the top half of their headlights painted black during World War II, because German submarines were sinking our ships.

Anyway, the Coast Guard patrol stopped them. She couldn't remember if they were on a horse or in a vehicle. They found out he was a poor fellow trying to get home and finally let him go.

Her daddy had a lot on the sound in Waterlily. After he made the deal for the house, he'd drive to Corolla and take apart a skiff load of the house. He didn't have a gas boat then, and somebody had let him use a skiff. He'd start poling that across the sound, and if he was lucky, some fisherman would see him and give him a tow to Waterlily. He kept doing that until he got the whole house over there, and he'd put it back together as he got it to Waterlily. Faye's daddy told me that himself. He told me something else I've never forgotten and have quoted many times: "There's nothing to it as long as you thoroughly understand it. Doesn't matter if it's going to the moon."

Grissie Barco was a very colorful character. He had a little railway for pulling up boats. He worked on boats, built boats and did a little fishing. He had a little round-stern gas boat when I knew him.

I remember one time when nylon line first came out, it was slick and would work itself loose if you didn't tie extra knots in it. My big hunting skiff with the float box on it was tied out to a stake out from Jones' Dock in Waterlily, which was just a few houses north of Grissie's house. One day, the wind was blowing strong northwest, and my skiff came untied and was heading for Corolla. Grissie saw it and went and got it with his gas boat. The next time he saw me, he told me, and I made sure I tied it up better after that.

Carova Beach

In 1967, George T. McLane and Jim Kabler and Associates bought the beach land that belonged to Currituck Gunning and Fishing Club on Knotts Island. Don't confuse this with Currituck Shooting Club at Poyner's Hill, which is said to be the oldest duck hunting club in America.

This tract of land joins Virginia and the Back Bay Wildlife Refuge. They started a subdivision and named it Carova Beach. This was the first development on Currituck beach. They had the lots platted out in the grid system. The lots were mostly 100 by 150 feet. They had some canals dug in from Knotts Island Bay on the sound side.

The property was selling primarily to people in Virginia Beach who wanted a place on the beach to come to. As there were no zoning regulations, many of the people who bought would have a single-wide house trailer pulled down there and set up on their lot.

Kabler & Riggs next bought a tract of beach property that joined Carova Beach to the south from Swan Island Club. They developed this in the same manner. By 1972, they had started developing the Whalehead property, which I've already told you about.

KAY COLE

Kay is the only sales agent for Kabler & Riggs who came down the beach from their office in Sandbridge to sell property in Carova Beach, Swan Beach and Whalehead that I know of. She is still in Corolla.

When Kabler & Riggs started developing and selling Carova Beach in 1967 or '68, Currituck County had no subdivision or zoning regulations.

The same thing was true when I started selling First Street (now Persimmon Street) in Corolla Village in 1970. By the time we got to Second and Third Streets, the county did have regulations.

Carova Beach and Corolla Village did have deed restrictions even though they were not required by the county. Kay said that Carova was intended to be a bedroom community for Virginia Beach, and quite a lot of the people that bought were from there.

It was their dream to have a beach house that they could get to in thirty or forty minutes. What price range are we talking about then? Originally there were lots in the $1,500 dollar range, maybe even less, and they would give discounts for multiple lots. It was sold by land contract. If you got it paid off, they'd give you a deed.

It wasn't much down at all. They did all the financing. Nobody would loan money on land back then. You couldn't even get money to build a house.

Kay said she moved to Sandbridge in 1972. Kay told me she is originally from Nashville, Tennessee, but she has lived in Corolla longer than anywhere else she has ever lived.

Kay got a job in Kabler & Riggs's rental department when she moved to Sandbridge. She managed that until she convinced them to let her sell down the beach.

Kay said:

> *I remember Sam Riggs said, "The next thing you know you'll want to sell down the beach." The guys up there didn't want to work on weekends and people were coming in there and wanting to buy property and nobody to help them. Up until this time there were just men selling in the four-wheel drive area.*
>
> *In 1978, I convinced them to let me sell, and they hired another woman. From then on, it just snowballed.*
>
> *In 1976, the U.S. Fish and Wildlife Service had closed the beach so that you couldn't drive through the Back Bay Wildlife Refuge. The only people that could get a pass to go through there were permanent old-time*

residents. Kabler & Riggs hired Gene Austin to come to Sandbridge every day to get the salespeople and take them to the property.

If Gene had gone with a salesperson and a client came in that wanted to see the property, the salesman had to call another permanent resident to come pick them up and had to negotiate a price, which the salesman had to pay.

Occasionally, somebody would come by boat and meet them at Carova Beach. The salesman still had to get Gene or another permanent resident to take him to meet the person coming by boat.

Ernie Bowden, Gene and Shirley Austin and Norris Austin were all very helpful to me. I knew you from Gene, Shirley and Norris. I knew you before you knew me.

It wasn't an easy thing to do to find a landmark. [That it wasn't. We marked tracts of land by old cars the ocean had taken, old refrigerators half covered up in the sand and things like that.] *Anytime you saw a house going up, if anybody was there, you went and knocked on the door and said what's your lot number? I made me a map that showed where the ramps were that you could get over the dune and tried to put some landmarks on the map. It was not easy finding the lots.*

As I said earlier, Kay is still in Corolla. She works for BD&A now. I see her in Corolla Chapel in the wintertime when Jo Ann and I are over there. Jo Ann has a house on Persimmon Street. She rents it in the summer, and we spend some weekends there in the winter and go to church at Corolla Chapel.

ERNIE BOWDEN

Cowboy of the Outer Banks

Ernie met me in Corolla on May 3, 2013. We had an hour-and-a-half taped conversation. At this time, Ernie is eighty-eight years old. He was born up around Penny's Hill or Lewark Hill, which ever you want to call it. He has lived most of his life on the northern Outer Banks. Ernie always wears his cowboy hat and boots.

Ernie said in the early days, everybody knew everybody on the Outer Banks. There weren't that many people over there. The basic revenues were commercial fishing and, until it was outlawed, commercial duck hunting.

Then folks became duck hunting guides or went into the Coast Guard, or they were livestock people:

Ernie Bowden was eighty-eight years old when I took this picture of him in Corolla. *Author's collection.*

> *One thing that's been overlooked for so many years is the livestock industry that existed on this Outer Banks. Dr. Baum bought Pine Island primarily for its grazing land for cattle. Then, the next people who had any cattle all lived in the village of Corolla.*
>
> *Captain Lewark had a herd of cattle after he retired from the Coast Guard. Mr. Callie Parker had a herd of cattle (he owned a little General Store right on Spry Creek). His father, old Mr. Hollis Parker, owned a tract of land, thirty-eight acres, right behind Seagull. Mr. Callie had a half brother, Elwood Parker, who married Captain Lewark's youngest daughter, Helen.*
>
> *When World War II started, a lot of people moved away from here. They went to the Currituck mainland, or they went south to Dare County where there was something going on, or they went to the tidewater area. There were very few people left here during World War II.*
>
> *Mr. Callie bought a piece of property on Poor Ridge in Kitty Hawk and moved his cattle down there. Captain Lewark died on his horse down there in the area known as the Three Sisters.* [three sand hills. As best I remember, they were on the Currituck Club property. I know if I had my float box tied out there in Morgan's Deep Water, I'd see geese sitting on those sand hills and hope something would come along and run them off.] *He was out looking for his cattle. Dark came, and he hadn't come home. His family and all the neighbors began looking for him. They didn't have anything but two-wheel drive*

vehicles, but they knew how to drive in the sand. They'd get up on those dunes and shine the headlights down in the grass. They found him. His horse had come home without him. He apparently died of a heart attack.

His herd got disbursed then. He had one son, Roy Lewark, who was in the real estate business in Virginia Beach, and a daughter who lived on the Currituck mainland—she married a Mr. Griggs from over there—and then another daughter, Helen, who married Elwood Parker.

The next herd of cattle was Mr. Lloyd O'Neal's He lived right up there north of the Monkey Island property a little bit.

The next herd was Mr. Leon White's He probably had the largest heard of cattle on the Outer Banks at that time. The next herd was my grandfather and uncle's.

The next herd was right up at the Virginia–North Carolina line: Mr. Linwood Dudley's He was Lee Dudley's nephew, the decoy carver whose ducks are so valuable today. Lee Dudley and Linwood's father were twins. Lee Dudley owned all that hunt club that was right on Munden's point just before you come on the causeway going to Knotts Island. The government owns it today. Jack Kitchen owned it at one time. When Mr. Lee Dudley died, his nephew Roy Dudley, who was a warrant officer in the Coast Guard, inherited that place, and Mr. Linwood Dudley inherited his father's place over on the beach. He owned all of Deal's Island. It was about four hundred acres of marshland with a couple of ponds in it as you went around the corner and back to his clubhouse that was on Dudley's Creek and Dudley's Island. The story went—I never placed much credence in it—but the story went that after a great big storm one time, a point of marsh had broken off up near the False Cape Hunt Club, which was two or three miles north of that, and had drifted down through Back Bay, and Mr. Linwood Dudley supposedly went out there and put some poles and stakes in it and anchored it. And it became known as Dudley's Island. This is in North Carolina, just before the state line.

The herdsmen had dipping vats they walked the cattle through to get the ticks and other bugs off them. Mr. Dudley's dipping vat is still up there right behind the Carova Beach property. Captain Lewark had a dipping vat right over here near where Buddy Ponton lives. Mr. Leon White had one almost in his yard. They used a mixture of sulphur, fish oil and water to dip them in. The U.S. Department of Agriculture started that program. Dipping vats were up and down the Outer Banks and on the Currituck mainland too. I can remember when I was about nine or ten years old, we'd go over to Mr. Leon White's place and drive a big herd of these cattle up *there, and a veterinarian had to be present. Dr. Fink from Elizabeth City would go over there. If we had a dog that had ticks on him, we threw him in there, too.*

"Yippi-yi-ay!" Big Roundup Along Beach Princess Anne Coastland Scene Reminiscent of Old West

Frank Blackford, Virginian Pilot *(Monday, August 15, 1949)*

Two Jeep loads of Princess Anne cowpunchers took off down the open beach yesterday for a roundup of a near-wild cattle herd below Virginia Beach.

The herd which roams inside a huge fenced area near the North Carolina line spent most of the spring and summer grazing on marsh and sea grass. With the cattle is a skittish herd of untamed horses, none of which has ever felt the weight of a man on its back.

Yesterday's roundup was a great success. Most of the cattle were penned by early afternoon. Three years ago, when the widely scattered animals were driven in, the men took three days to find them all.

Like the great West. After the six a.m. start, the cow punchers stopped first at the home of Linwood Dudley, about twenty miles below Virginia Beach. Dudley was out trying to locate the cattle in the heavy rain when the men arrived. They waited for him on the wide veranda of his home that looked almost like something out of the old west with mounted cattle and deer horns every few feet along the porch.

Four of the cowpunchers, Jack Etheridge, a farmer; Albert Atwood, a farmer; William Malbon, a farmer; his cousin, Jack Malbon, a beef cattle man, set off on horseback to drive the herd to a pen of Lonnie Bowden's about eight miles below the Dudley place.

Just before the horsemen set off, J.J. Waterfield, caretaker of the False Cape Club, whose grandfather had cut grass on these same marshes to feed his cattle, joined the party with his son, J.J. Jr., A few months before Waterfield's old milk cow and her calf had gotten out of her pasture and had joined the herd. He wanted them back.

The men on horseback set off through the wet scrub pine and live oak after the cattle. The other men in two Jeeps, started down the beach, hunting cows as sea gulls wheeled overhead and a line of wild geese rose from a marsh.

Cattle Found Near Beach

The cattle were spotted first near the beach where they had come during the night to get cool from the sea breeze and to escape the bugs and mosquitoes in the marsh.

The men in Jeeps, D.J Craft, plumber, "Boots" Ames, engineer, and Dick Etheridge, a farmer joined in helping to bring in the cattle.

The cattle came splashing through the pools of rainwater back of the beach, led by a wild-maned spotted brown mare with her tan colt galloping at her side. The horsemen created a sand dune and swooped down at the lowing cattle in the distance. A Jeep circled out to head off the cattle on the other flank. The drive was on now in earnest.

"Hey, hey, hey!" a horseman shouted, riding somewhat incongruously in hip boots, "Punch 'em up. Drive those strays back into the herd."

Over the sound of the pounding hooves floated the whine of an outboard motor and the raucous squawk of a marsh hen.

Runs Over Wild Sow

Billy Malbon shouted to one of the men in the Jeep as he passed that he "ran over a wild sow in the bushes. She turned three summersaults landed on her feet and kept running."

The men drove the cattle on in Bowden's half open gate. The coral fence was ringed with onlookers including children from the small settlement of Penny's Hill where Dudley lives.

A sand fiddler scurried for safety as the bellowing cattle shoved and pushed their way in the pen. Back of the corral was an old wrecked plane pontoon which held grain for the livestock. About forty cattle were driven into the enclosure. The horses all escaped.

Then the culling out began. Bowden, the two Etheridge's and Albert Atwood slipped into the pen with the plunging cattle and drove out the larger ones. Only the calves that were headed for market were left.

As a wild black heifer, breathing hard and obviously ready for trouble, tossed her head and started for the men they jumped her. Atwood was kicked in the chest, but they caught the animal, checked her identifying ear notches, and culled her out of the bunch.

When the herd was down to only a few cattle, the men had some difficulty with the skittish animals.

"Let's get some of this wild stuff out of here. I'm afraid of it," someone shouted.

WILD ONE LASSOED

The cowpunchers had trouble, too, with another little black heifer who was supposed to go to market. She stayed in the dense pack of cattle until Billy Malbon, after several tries, lassoed her. The animal reared up on her hind legs, pawing at the air as the men jumped for the fence. Once inside the stake body truck the heifer bellowed with fear and rage and almost plunged completely over the cab until she was stopped.

Finally when the roundup was over, someone suggested a swim in the ocean.

Bowden, who fishes and hunts as well as punches cattle, grinned and shook his head.

"I haven't been swimming lately," he said. "Friday I saw three sharks—big man eaters eight or ten feet long in close to shore. Two were at the breakers and one was inside."

No one went swimming. The party, with the day's work over, headed for the home of W.L. Cogswell, at whose summer home, "Oak Hollow," a barbeque was being prepared.

The day before the roundup, several of the men had come down and butchered a wild goat which was to be barbequed by an expert, George Wadsworth, secretary of the Builders and Contractors Exchange, Inc. The slow cooking took eight hours over an open pit. Wadsworth's son, George helped in the cattle drive.

All during the roundup Wadsworth with two Negro helpers, had been cooking the meat over oak coals, basting it from time to time with a hot pepper and vinegar sauce. The barbeque was at six o'clock.

Cogsworth, who works in Norfolk, said it had been a perfect day with one small exception.

"After they skinned that goat", he said, "I spread the hide out and rubbed salt into it. I thought I might have myself a goatskin rug. Well just about daybreak I heard an awful noise outside. One of these wild hogs had my goatskin in his mouth and the rest of the herd was right on his heels. So that was the end of my rug."

CATTLE OWNERS

Ernie named all the cattle owners from Dare County to Sandbridge, Virginia. I just included the ones on Currituck beach. He said he didn't know any cattle owners on Hatteras Island, but he did on Ocracoke. He said in 1931, the State of North Carolina passed what it referred to as the fence law. I guess it was the WPA (Works Progress Administration, which Franklin D. Roosevelt started in the Depression to give people a job) that was setting out beach grass to stabilize the dunes, and the legislators thought the cattle were destroying it.

I do remember the first time I ever went to Nags Head. Mama, Daddy and I had a wreck with a cow. I was a very little boy, and I just remember it was at night.

SHEEP

The livestock industry was a big thing on the Outer Banks, particularly Currituck County. The livestock industry extended beyond cattle; we had sheep as well, large flocks of sheep. The bugger man in the hayloft were dogs, pet dogs. If a dog ever gets killing sheep—same thing with chickens—if he ever gets to killing chickens, it's bad. Dogs were the big problem with raising sheep. The livestock industry in Currituck has never really received the recognition it probably should have.

HORSES

How about the horses Ernie? Tell me about the horses:

Prior to World War II, a lot of people on this beach had horses. Mr. Pell Austin had a horse. He lived over there in what's now Jim Scarborough's house. He was in the Coast Guard, and he'd ride it on patrol. Everybody in the neighborhood had a horse. Captain Lewark had a horse he looked after his cattle with. Everybody's yard was fenced in. People used them for transportation, to pull horse carts and visited neighbors.

When I was a child, my dad used to ride a horse all the time when he was on patrol. He was stationed down here on the beach. Lots of times, if he had the first patrol of an evening, he had an old horse called Sunny-boy; that horse was the same age I was. My grandmother owned the mare, and she gave the colt to my dad. He hooked that horse to the cart, and my mother and sister and brother and I in the summertime would ride with him on that patrol. The cart had a little seat up front; then, it had a little space behind it and a backboard to drop in at the back of the cart.

He'd drive the horse and cart all the way down to what they called a check post in those days. Each Coast Guard station had brass medallion things about the size of a quarter or half dollar. There was a check post with a box on it half way between the Washwoods station and the False Cape station, a distance of three miles. The False Cape Patrol would pick up Washwoods medallions and vice versa. At the end of every week, they would replace those things. They called them checks. This was the same way all down the beach between Coast Guard stations.

Later on, they went to a dial clock they had to punch in a certain time frame. You had a thirty-minute leeway in there, or you were in trouble with the officer in charge.

The Coast Guard did away with a lot of the Coast Guard stations in 1937. Currituck Beach station, Penny's Hill, Paul Gamell Hill and False Cape were not active; Wash Woods, Little Island, Caffey's Inlet, Kitty Hawk, Kill Devil Hills and Nags Head all stayed active.

When World War II started, they reactivated some of the deactivated stations and established a horse patrol. The cavalry in the army became mechanized. They did away with all the horse-drawn cannons and all that stuff. They had all these horses, so they sent a bunch of them to these Coast Guard stations. The old lighthouse keeper's house right here in Corolla was stacked full of hay. You could hardly walk in any one of the rooms. They kept hay there for the Washwoods station and Currituck Beach, too.

They used to show movies in the old original boathouse behind Currituck Beach station. We used to come down here from Penny's Hill and watch a movie. A lot of the girls from the Currituck mainland worked over here at the Whalehead Club after Mr. Adams got it and leased it to the Coast Guard.

When the war was over, everybody at these stations was given an opportunity to have one of the horses if you wanted it. There was a horse here at Currituck Beach with a white streak in his face named Major. The Coast Guard gave him to Max Gray, and Major used to get up there with my horses. Raymond Williams, who was stationed at Washwoods, kept a big black gelding. All the rest of the horses they gathered up and took them up to Princess Anne Hunt Club right next door to the Cavalier Hotel on the hill and auctioned them off. I went to that sale. I guess I was about twenty years old then. All those army horses had a serial number branded underneath their mane.

Originally, every horse on this beach was owned by somebody. Dr. Baum had brought a stallion here. In my mind, I seem to recall he got him in Oklahoma. He sold Mr. Roy O'Neal a colt that was sired by that horse. He was a nice quarter horse. Mr. Roy kept him a stud and broke and rode him; herded up cattle with him. Everybody who had a mare used that stud.

In the late summer when all the sheep and cattle herding was over, Mr. Lloyd would take that horse up there in the salt marsh around the big Hay Pond and the Endicott Pond on the Swan Island Hunt Club property and turn him loose up there, and everybody else did the same thing. They didn't have any use for their horses until the summer. There would be about maybe a dozen horses up there. Spring of the year would come and Mr. Lloyd would be ready to start looking after his cattle again. He had an old 1933 or '34 model Ford pickup truck. Back then, it wasn't grown up like it is now. There were so few trees, you could stand out there to the ocean and almost see Knotts Island Bay. The overwash kept anything from growing. Anyway, Mr. Lloyd would go up there with a ten-quart water bucket with corn in it, and he'd see that horse out there, three or four hundred yards out there, in the marsh. He'd walk as close to the marsh as he could and shake that bucket, and the horse would come right up there to him.

Mr. Lloyd would put a rope around his neck. He didn't have anything like a halter in those days. He'd tie him to the tailgate of the pickup, the horse would follow him home and he'd keep him home all summer. I bought the last real native horse, a mare, on this beach from Mr. Charlie Waterfield. She had a filly that died; she was by the same stud that Mr. Lloyd had. That stud died when he was about twenty-two years old. They said he died from eating sand spurs, but I think they were just picking on anything. Age got him as much as anything.

My uncle had the last foal that horse had, and I had next to the last foal. I gave Mr. Charlie Waterfield thirty-five dollars for the mare and the foal. The old mare, gosh, she was between twenty-five and twenty-eight years old I reckon when she had that last foal. I broke that filly and used her getting up cattle.

What few horses were here were owned. My uncle had two, and I had three horses at that time. It was right after World War II. Most of the horses were gone except the ones that my dad, my uncle and I owned.

ERNIE BOWDEN ON CAROVA BEACH

Jim Kabler, of Kabler Realty, developed Sandbridge and was about to run out of land.

Mr. George T. McLean and Jim Culbreath bought the beach property of Currituck Gunning and Fishing Club. They owned it fifty-fifty in 1954. In 1967, Jim Kabler approached Jim Culbreath, who had in the meantime moved up to New York, and purchased his 50 percent of the property for $1 million. He came back and approached Mr. McLean to develop the property jointly and call it Carova Beach. They formed two corporations. Carova Beach was Mr. McLean's corporation, and Ocean Sands (not to be confused with James Johnson's Ocean Sands) was Jim Kabler and his associates' part. They combined corporations and called it the Carova Corporation.

The development proceeded from 1967 until 1972, and it includes some 2,300 residential lots, covering three and a half miles of oceanfront.

Sam Riggs was a dentist. He joined up with Kabler in 1969 and formed Kabler & Riggs Realty.

Carova Beach, 1970s. *Author's collection.*

BEACH PONIES

There were two brothers from Virginia Beach who I went to school with in old Princess Anne County. I rode a school bus up that beach for years back when my dad was stationed at Washwoods and False Cape. The two brothers were Dallas (we called him Pete) and the other one was Elmo (we called him Piggy). Their last name was Hogge. Pete was a magistrate in the city of Virginia Beach. Piggy had an automobile repair business. Pete had married old man Leon White's granddaughter, Commie White's daughter.

They were getting ready to build that old Route 44, a toll road that cut Virginia Beach in half. They were buying the land and moving the houses away. There was a guy down in Pungo named Steve Fentress. Steve and Piggy both bought two of those small houses, and they brought them down there and put 'em on the Leon White tract. Steve Fentress moved them down the beach for them. They were little two-bedroom, one-bath houses, maybe six or seven hundred square feet. The rest of the heirs didn't like it. It got so tough on them that Pete and Piggy bought two lots back there on Ocean Pearl road in Carova Beach and had those houses moved again.

Pete had two ponies—a little stud and a mare that his boy rode—and he had brought them down there to the Leon White place when he moved that house down there.

The rest of the family didn't like Pete or Margaret, old man Leon White's granddaughter, or her brother Ray. He got killed over there somewhere around Point Harbor, and I don't think they ever found out who killed him.

But anyway, they moved those ponies up there on that lot they had moved the house to. They fenced up a place in the pine trees (there's a fence right there today) and put those two ponies in there and left them there. They'd come down the beach on weekends. He had a bathtub in the place and he'd fill that up with water and put a bale of hay out there for them. Sometimes he'd come back the next weekend and sometimes he didn't, and the things got to where they were about to starve to death. So we just went down there one weekend and opened the gate and turned them loose.

The next horse let loose belonged to the son of Mr. Linwood Dudley (owner of the Dudley Hunt Club)—Garland. She was a little mare, and the old man could ride her, but his feet nearly dragged the ground.

They sold that hunt club and didn't hunt down there anymore. He was in the Merchant Marines anyway. [His brother was captain of the ocean liner United States. There were three of those boys, and Oswell was the captain of the United States when she set the speed record for crossing the Atlantic Ocean, a record that still stands today. It was Oswell, Garland and Leon Dudley.]

Anyway, he turned that little mare a loose when he left the beach. Those three ponies are the beginning of what you see here on this beach today. That's exactly what they are, and they have multiplied and multiplied and gotten to be a big nuisance and danger here in the Corolla area. The roads have been paved, and there is a lot of traffic here.

Gerald Friedman furnished all the material, and got a fence put up from the sound to out in the ocean and put that cattle guard in there where the road crosses to keep those horses out of Corolla. Now they are all up there on the north end.

Twice to my knowledge they have gathered up a bunch of them and sold them. Some of the women down here in Corolla, Debbie Westner and some others, kinda took it upon themselves to look after those ponies. One of the women used to work for the county at the satellite office here.

I don't know how many I've killed. I've lost track of it, but they'd call me once every month or two when traffic was heavy in the tourist season and say, "Come down here and kill this horse a car has hit and get rid of it."

Debbie and the other folks gathered up at one time seventeen of those horses in my corral and gave them to a man from Smithfield, North Carolina. He came up here with two big stock trailers and hauled them away.

Another time they gathered up nine; I think those ponies went out toward Raleigh, but that's what the horses are all about.

Ernie During World War II

Ernie, were you ever in the Coast Guard?

No, I lost half my right foot in a fire when I was only two months old. The Coast Guard wouldn't have me.

During World War II, my dad got transferred to New York as the boat officer at the Manhattan Beach Coast Guard Training Station. I graduated from high school in June, and he got transferred in up there in December right after Pearl Harbor; as soon as school was out, my family and I moved up to New York. I went to school there at Brooklyn Tech and studied trigonometry and advanced algebra so I could enter Pratt Institute and study engineering, and I worked at night for Sperry Gyroscope Corporation in the inspection of bombsites and antiaircraft gun sights. That's what I did during the war.

After the war was over, I came back down to Oceana where I had gone to school from first grade through high school.

The first year I went to school, I didn't have any transportation off the beach. I had an uncle and aunt, Roy and Frances Lewark (old Mr. Ike Gallop's daughter down there in Harbinger). They lived in Oceana. I started school when I was five years old, and I lived there with them that year. I came home on weekends. Dad and Mother would come up there and get me, and I'd spend the weekend at home. If the weather was bad, sometimes I didn't get home for a couple or three weeks, but I lived there with them through the first grade.

The next year, Captain Roy Dudley's wife drove their two sons and me to Oceana to school every day.

In the third grade, the old Princess Anne County established a school bus service to the area down on the beach known as Washwoods. They contracted with a resident down that way, Walter Waterfield's son, Phillip. He bought an old Dodge truck and the school system up there furnished the school bus body. It would hold about fifteen children. It was an old two-wheel drive truck. We all rode that bus from then on until they closed the Coast Guard station. My dad was transferred then to Cape Henry, then to Little Creek and then to Kill Devil Hills. I spent two summers down there with him in 1940 and '41. Then the war started in December 1941.

I worked for Little Jethro Midgett when I was fourteen and fifteen years old. You could get your driver's license then when you were fourteen years old. Little Jethro had lost his driver's license (I think there was some drinking involved). He had a fish-packing and seafood business next door to his mother's store, just south of the casino in Nags Head.

My job was putting ice in iceboxes. Everybody had iceboxes down there in those days because electricity was off more than it was on. I had a route from the First Colony Inn to the Nags Head Coast Guard station. Bill Mann's route was from Nags Head Coast Guard station to South Nags Head. Horatio and Elwood Culpepper had everything from the First Colony Inn up to where Lindsey Dowdy's place was (where the Kitty Hawk Fishing Pier is today). Those were the three ice routes. I got paid fifty cents a day and my lunch. I ate the same thing everyday in Miss Mattie's store (that was Jethro's mother): a can of potted meat, a little box of saltine crackers and a Coca Cola. I didn't work Saturdays and Sundays.

On Sundays, I'd usually go in the woods and shoot bullfrogs with a rifle and sell the legs to the hotels, and I'd catch soft crabs when the moon was right and sell them to the hotels. I got sixty cents a dozen for soft crabs, and they had to be as big as my hand before they'd buy them; I got sixty cents a dozen for frogs. That would be two dozen frog legs. I lived in that building that Doug Twiddy has for a real estate office. That was the original Kill Devil Hills station, and Doug Twiddy moved it to Corolla. It was out there on the beach a little bit south of the station that's there now. The Coast Guard had made an apartment up stairs in that old thing for Commander C.J. Sullivan. He was commander of the seventh Coast Guard district, and he would go down there sometimes on vacation. It had gotten to where he hardly ever came. I couldn't stay in the Coast Guard station with my dad, but I could stay in that apartment.

Doug has artifacts in there now. I've given him several things, like one of those magneto crank telephones that the Coast Guard used to have. They gave me all that stuff out of the Washwoods Coast Guard station. My dad and I leased it for twenty-two years from the Coast Guard. I operated a hunt club there on the five hundred acres I'd bought from Bill Trent, Currituck Gunning and Fishing Club.

To back up a little bit, Mr. Trent bought the False Cape Hunt Club property (five and a half miles of oceanfront and all the marsh) for $2,300. This included all the decoys, two hunting batteries and everything else. He bought it in 1932, and he sold it in 1938 to Colonel Slover of Landmark Communications. Slover adopted a fellow named Frank Batten, who inherited it all.

Mr. Trent then came down there and bought the Currituck Gunning and Fishing Club property for $8,900. This is now Carova Beach. Mr. Trent had three partners in that thing. Bill Webb, owner of Tazewell Garage; Joe Addington, owner of Addington-Beamon Lumber Company; and Riley Borem, who owned a big pharmaceutical business.

Mr. Trent had a neighbor named Hartwell Gary, who owned Gary Steel. He made underground tanks. Gary bought the five hundred acres from Mr. Trent that Mr. Trent got from me, and he gave Mr. Trent the same $8,500 for that five hundred acres that Mr. Trent had given for the whole Currituck Gunning and Fishing Club property: three and a half miles of oceanfront from the ocean to Knotts Island and the clubhouse on Knotts Island. Hartwell Gary kept it through the war. He was doing a lot of government contracting. He was using that place to bring contractors and officers down there to get on the good side of them.

Hartwell had a little boy that got drowned in a swimming pool at his house after the war was over. He lived in a high-dollar area in Norfolk. His wife never wanted to live there any longer after the boy's death.

Since Gary Steel had a big plant up in Lynchburg, Virginia, Hartwell moved his wife up there. I called him to see if he wanted to sell that five hundred acres. I had just sold my refrigeration and air-conditioning business, which I'd gotten into just after the war. He told me to come to his office and he'd talk with me. I sat down there with him, and he said he'd take just what he paid for it. I went back over there and counted him out eighty-nine $100 bills. Same thing he had paid for it. The same thing Mr. Trent had paid for the whole Currituck Gunning and Fishing Club property. This was everything from the Virginia line down to the Swan Island property. This five hundred acres is part of what is now Carova Beach.

[Don't confuse Currituck Gunning and Fishing Club at Knotts Island with Currituck Shooting Club at Poyner's Hill, which I talked about in the first of this book.]

This property is right behind the Washwoods Coast Guard station. My dad and I leased that from the Coast Guard for twenty years and had a hunt club there.

I never knew that. What was the name of the club?

It never had a name until Kroghie Andresen wrote that book, Gunning Birds; *he named it Bowden Club. I had some real good club members, some doctors and some lawyers, and Mr. G.M. Blake was a member of my club up there. I don't know what he didn't own. He could hardly read or write, but he was discharged after World War I in Norfolk, and he went to work in the army base out there firing the boiler that heated the army base. He worked the night shift. Automobiles were just coming along then after World War I, and he learned to do body and fender work, straightening fenders on model A Fords and all those things. When he passed away, Mr. Blake owned stock in the Pine Island Ferries, in the Virginia Ferry Corporation and the Norfolk County Ferry System. When they built tunnels in place of all those ferries and built the Chesapeake Bay Bridge Tunnel, they gave him stock in all those tunnels in exchange for his stock in the ferries.*

Mr. Blake owned at least seven taxi-cab companies in Norfolk.

We got to be good friends, and he took a membership with me. I charged members $2,000 a year, and I took in ten members. They had the use of the Coast Guard station. There were four bedrooms upstairs, and one bedroom downstairs. They could bring their families down in the summer for a weekend or more. They had to arrange for whoever was coming when.

I had a good group of people from Richmond. Jack Broader, an attorney, and Wyatt B. Corneal. They stayed with me as long as I operated it. I quit operating it in 1962. I turned it all over to my dad. I was concentrating on my cattle herd. I leased all the Swan Island marsh down to what we called Big Fluffy's. My uncle leased from there on down to about where the Parker tract, the Leon White tract, was.

The president of Swan Island Club that I negotiated a lease with was Edwin Arnold. He was a fine person, and I kept that lease with him until they sold it. I leased all that marshland and fenced it all. It was eleven miles of barbed-wire fence.

In 1966, I bought a small herd of cattle from Lundy Cason's wife (Lundy had been manager of Swan Island Hunt Club). I got a barge from Mr. George Twiford at Monkey Island. It had been sunk there for years. Mr. George had said, "You're welcome to it, Ernie, if you can get her up." It was full of mud and everything. It was about twenty-four feet long, all juniper. I caught the tide real low and went down there with a pump and pumped her out and darned if I didn't break her loose, and she came to the top.

I had a gas boat that my dad had Carl Beasley over at Poplar Branch build. She had a seven-inch tunnel in her and would run in shallow water. I towed the barge over to Old Inlet with that and put it on the shore and caulked all the seams. I had to put some new deck on it. I built a pen on her.

I took her out there to Swan Island and got those old cattle on that barge and brought them to the beach.

I bought everybody's cattle on the beach. I bought Mr. Linwood Dudley's herd, Lunnie's herd; even old man Johnny Waterfield had three cows, and I bought them.

I took the pen off that old barge and started putting in some bulkheads. I put in part of a bulkhead for Mr. George Twiford down there at Monkey Island on the east side.

Then I had Mr. Wilton Walker build me a big barge. I hauled feed from Knotts Island. I rented farmland over there from different people and raised corn and hay for my cattle. I hauled hay and grain from Knotts Island for several years with that barge. Then, I started buying peanut residue from Birdsong up in Suffolk. I was buying that stuff for a half cent a pound when I first started buying it.

I sold that barge to a guy up in Virginia that had a liquor still on an island out there in Back Bay, and he was using it to haul sugar and whatever else he used out there.

I knew him real good, and he used it for several years. He owned a grocery store up there around Pungo. He was running the sugar through the grocery store. He had a guy named Robert Henley, old man Amos Henley's son, running the still for him. Robert was hauling a load of somethin' out there on that barge one night and somehow he fell overboard and drowned. By that time, the ATF had gotten a hold of it, and they went down there and blew the still up. They didn't catch anybody at the still, but that barge served its purpose.

Didn't you have a buffalo over there at one time? Where did you get the buffalo?

Yeah. I bought five to start with from Billy Malbon up there in Virginia Beach, and then I bought some from up in Harrisonburg, Virginia. I bought two or three from R.A. Hoy, the air-conditioning man, and I bought two or three from up in Maryland somewhere. At one time, I had fifteen. I sold all of them when I sold my cattle.

In the 1930s, Swan Island Hunt Club and the Currituck Gunning and Fishing Club on Knotts Island filed a lawsuit concerning the north end of the beach that required people to lay claim to their property. It essentially said, "If you claim ownership of any land within the boundaries between the north boundary of the Currituck Inlet, the west boundary of the Currituck Sound, the east boundary of the Atlantic Ocean and an undescribed south boundary, come forth now and prove your claim or forever hold your peace." This process calls only for public advertisement, and of course, these people on the beach didn't know anything about it. They had no contact with the courthouse back in those days—no telephone, radio or anything.

A lot of people just had little parcels of land. There was a piece of property known as the James White patent; it was a land grant. A good many people had purchased parts of that or inherited it. There was a lady from Churches Island, Miriam Jarvis, who owned four and a half acres of the old James White patent, and she didn't get to defend it. There was another lady, whose name I can't remember. Then there was Mr. Thomas O'Neal. Another was Miss Lavinia Melson (Richard and Mitt Melson's mother). They lost it all because they didn't know anything about it.

They all moved away. Richard went in the Coast Guard. Mr. Thomas O'Neal died and didn't have any heirs. I never knew much about the Jarvises on the mainland. I just knew her first name was Miriam. Apparently, she didn't have any knowledge of what was going on.

All that land that was in those boundaries became Swan Island property. The only person who defended his ownership was old man Leon White. He had a brother named Bode White, and he owned land down there where Lun Green Island, northeast of Monkey Island, is. Mr. Leon owned Big Skinner's Island, Mosey Oak's Pond and Bushey Island, the home place. They were the only two that defended their property.

Mr. Leon White had eleven children. The oldest one was named Ross. He got killed in World War I. He never had any children. All the rest of them had children. The last time I had a count on it, there were over seventy heirs to the Leon White Estate, and every one of them has been contacted by two different groups: the Meredith boy or Whit Sessoms and Jim Braithwaite. They have bought up parts of that thing now. I don't know anybody of the old Leon White heirs except those fellows from Wanchese, Bobby and Sam Dough. Mr. Leon White had two daughters who married people from Wanchese. Cloey married a man named Tillett (Pete and Leland were her sons). The other one married the Dough fellow. He owns some property up there on the north end of Roanoke Island, around Fort Raleigh. Those are the only people I know of the original Whites who still own any interest in the L.R. White Estate. Commie's wife and son Ray sold their whole interest to Tom Broyles and Tommy Crooks, who used to work with Mr. Elijah Tate from Coinjock.

Old man Leon White had a little piece of land right up in the middle of the Swan Island property up there around the big hay ponds. I think it was twenty-three acres of it, and the rest of the family at that time agreed to let Commie's wife, Katherine, and her children have that free and clear for her interest in all the four hundred and some acres of the main home place.

When they got title to that, they sold it to Tom Broyles. He was an attorney. Then, Tom Broyles and his group (Tommy Crooks, Tom Broyles, Tom Les Disharoon and Dippy Pender) ended up buying all of the Swan Island Hunt Club property. They were big in the insurance business.

They sold what today is Swan Beach around 1970. Gerald Friedman, Sam and Harry Sandler and Isadore Schwartz bought Swan Beach.

They divided the Swan Island oceanfront up into three equal parts. Six thousand and some feet in Swan Beach, six thousand and some feet in North Swan Beach and six thousand and some feet in the middle tract.

The Friedman group bought Swan Beach first; then, they bought North Swan Beach. [The middle tract ended up being sold to the Nature Conservancy at the same time they bought the Monkey Island property, which U.S. Fish and Wildlife has today.]

But first, Gerald and that group bought it. They bought Swan Beach and then North Swan Beach, and then they bought the middle third. That's when the interest rates went sky high, in the mid-1970s. It got up to 21 percent. The banks started calling in all the notes. Gerald went to Israel and came back with $12 or $13 million and paid off the banks, but they defaulted on their notes to Tom Broyles's group, and the land went back. They got the middle piece back. When they defaulted, some of the principals were the same ones that were in North Swan Beach. Gerald Friedman and his group insisted that Tom Broyles and all of 'em deed to them a one-hundred-foot right of way that would connect Swan Beach with North Swan Beach, and that one-hundred-foot right of way was deeded and recorded and is in the Register of Deeds office today. Today, there is a power line laid on that same right of way from Swan Beach to North Swan Beach.

Prior to that time, all Carova Beach and North Swan Beach got their power from Virginia.

Gerald and all of them had enough foresight that they knew that those two pieces needed to be connected with a right of way. Now everything even up into Virginia gets power from North Carolina. They laid a 4,400-volt underground cable from Swan Beach to North Swan Beach.

Which piece of property is that big twenty-three bedroom house R.V. Owens has on?

That's the north part of the middle tract. Cunningham Gray was one of the owners of the Swan Island Club along with Dippy Pender and all the rest of them when they bought it. Horace Gray was a big, big timber man. He owned a big part of Continental Can and Timber. He was also a part of the state legislature for a long time. The Gray family up in Wakefield, Virginia, and around that area is where the Gray family is strong. When Friedman's group defaulted, Horace Gray and Mr. Cunningham got that piece of property that R.V. now has; they deeded it to Virginia Military Institute, and they were the trustees for it. They sold it to R.V. Owens. That piece of property runs from the ocean straight back to Knotts Island Bay.

R.V. subdivided it into ten-acre tracts to get around local restrictions. In doing that the oceanfront was the thing they were interested in. They had to add in all that marsh to make up ten acres. They would have a little piece of high ground on the oceanfront, but they'd have seven or eight acres of marsh behind it to go with this oceanfront to make the ten acres. That's how they subdivided it.

Later on, Dippy Pender, Tom Broyles and all sold to the Nature Conservancy.

The Nature Conservancy did not buy the Currituck Gunning and Fishing Club marsh. Fish and Wildlife bought it out and out. Mr. Trent developed cancer, and they all got together and sold it before he died. They sold it to Atlantic and Gulf Stevedores, and they later sold it to the Fish and Wildlife Service, except the clubhouse and the land around it on Knotts Island.

MIDWIFE

Faye Barco Hooper told me she was born over here on Spry Creek, and she said the midwife that delivered her was named Margaret "Lady Bug" Bowden. Was that your mother?

That was my grandmother. She delivered children up and down this beach. She raised Doc Fulcher and his sister Robana, and then she raised three of Robana's children. Faye told me that Margaret Bowden's name is on her birth certificate.

Both of my grandmothers were from Dare County. My grandmother "Lady Bug," as everybody called her, was a Beasley. Her father's name was Billy Beasley, and he had a brother named Lem Beasley. They were from Nags Head.

Her mother was Mr. Cecil O'Neal's sister, named Charity O'Neal. She married my grandmother's father, Billy Beasley. When my grandmother was ten years old, Charity died. Either she had a sister or my grandmother's daddy, Billy Beasley, had a sister that lived on Knotts Island.

In 1888, my great-grandfather brought my grandmother in a horse and cart from Nags Head up here to what is Wash Woods Coast Guard station and met her aunt and uncle on the bayside over there, and she lived with them until she got married. She married my grandfather of course, Bill Bowden. Same name as my dad. She told me when they got to Currituck

Inlet, they had to wait for low tide to get across that inlet with that horse and cart. That was the new Currituck Inlet. The old Currituck Inlet was at the Virginia North Carolina line.

That was another thing about this Outer Banks. The beginning of North Carolina is right there on that beach, at the north end of Carova Beach. I don't know if you have ever seen that monument or not. The number one monument that started that separated the state of North Carolina from Virginia sits right up there in that woods at the north end of Carova Beach.

I went by that thing when I was seven or eight years old herding up sheep. The kids had to crawl under the bushes to run the sheep out where the men couldn't get with horses. Crawl in there under the briers, vines and everything. The sheep would go in there to hide. We used to drive those things right on down past that monument to Mr. Linwood Dudley's dipping vat. That's about a half a mile south of that monument. The only way that monument could have been located there is they brought it in by barge. It's made of granite. It was cut somewhere in the mountains. That thing stands more than six feet tall.

It's the only place in the whole country that I've ever been that I've ever seen the state of North Carolina spelled, capital N.Ca., and it's engraved in that monument up there. On one side of it is N.Ca., and the other side is Virginia.

When I was on the board of commissioners, I had the good fortune to meet with a professor from the University of Virginia at one of these hurricane conferences that I used to attend every year.

He had done an awful lot of research on coastal storms and told me that there were two big storms, one was in March 1846 and the other was in September 1847. He said that Henry Ansell Beasley, who's buried in a cemetery just south of Ryland Poyner's auto repair shop in Barco, wrote an unpublished manuscript describing his eyewitness account. It's on file at UNC at Chapel Hill, and it's on file at the Currituck County Library.

He described that storm. He said that ocean waters were breaking on the east shore of Knotts Island, and that livestock and parts of houses and things were washing up on the shore over there.

Ever since I could remember there was an area where we developed Carova Beach, right south of section three as you are coming into section four was always quicksand. If you drove an automobile out in there and had much rain that summer, you'd fall right in. There were some pieces of stumps that sat up just above the sand in the grass. If you ran over one of those things, you'd ruin a tire. I started digging those canals up there, and

I'd run into trees that had been pushed over and were lying flat and covered with sand. I'm sure that happened in one of those storms.

COUNTY COMMISSIONER

Last but not least, Ernie Bowden was a Currituck County Commissioner, elected by the people of this county for twenty-four years.

Ernie and I are both nearing the end of life's journey. We both know a lot firsthand about how Currituck Beach used to be and both saw it developed as it is today, and we had a part in its early development, as you have already read in this book.

I felt that we should put to print the firsthand knowledge we have of Currituck Beach before that knowledge is gone forever.

We would like for future generations to know what Currituck Beach used to be like.

I hope you have enjoyed the book, and I hope future generations will help keep Currituck Beach the beautiful place it is today.

The stories in this book that I and others have told are true and correct to the best of our memory and recollection; however, we assume no liability for its accuracy.

About the Author

Travis Morris was born in Coinjock, North Carolina, in 1932 (in the same house his mother was born in on April 3, 1903). He was the only child of Chester and Edna Boswood Morris. His father was an attorney and later a superior court judge. While practicing law, Judge Morris represented many of the old hunt clubs in Currituck County, which is how Travis came by much of his firsthand knowledge. These hunt clubs owned nearly all of Currituck Beach from the late 1800s up until the beginning of development in 1968. Travis served three years in the U.S. Coast Guard and then spent a year and a half at Campbell College. Early on, he farmed and had a long-distance trucking company; he also guided sportsmen and managed Monkey Island Hunting Lodge. In 1983, he cofounded Piney Island Club with John High, which is still in existence and of which he is still a member. For the past forty-three years, he has been in the real estate business.

Travis served on the Currituck County Planning Board for eight years and has been a member of the Currituck County Historical Society for as long as he can remember. Even though he has been writing recollections for pleasure for many years, he never dreamed he would have eight books published. But he has thoroughly enjoyed sharing the memories with the public.